LIFE AT THE ANGEL'S

❧ NEST ❧

NURSING

HOME

To God be the Glory!

Shirley Marshall

Sam Mym

ISBN 978-1-63885-765-5 (Paperback)
ISBN 978-1-63885-766-2 (Digital)

Covenant Books, Inc.
11661 Hwy 707
Murrells Inlet, SC 29576
www.covenantbooks.com

True accounts with changes in names to protect the guilty!

My bucket list is almost complete. Writing this book will complete it. I want to dedicate my first book to the many residents at the Angel's Nest Nursing Home, who gave me the incredible stories; to my loving husband, who encouraged me to finish what I had started; my dear friend Bud, who has gone to be with the Lord but, while here, challenged me to write this book; to our five children and grands that call us Pop and Mym; to my precious momma, who gave me the title for this book by always saying I was living in a "nest of angels" that have Momma with them up in heaven; and, most of all, to the Lord above for letting me work there for twenty-five years and live to tell these unique and fun adventure stories to the world!

CONTENTS

PREFACE

Twenty-five years ago, the Lord led me to a fabulous nursing home to work. At the time, I had been in sales and traveled nine months out of the year with little time to be normal. My college roommate told me there was an opening at this wonderful place, so when I came home one week, it was imperative to find this interesting home for the elderly. After three interviews with a Catholic sister and praying for a sign from God, I was called on my birthday and offered the position of activity director for independent living at the Angel's Nest Nursing Home, which I will refer to as the Nest. The time spent there was the most rewarding and the most exciting time of my life, except for the times I gave birth to two wonderful boys and married my soulmate at age forty-seven.

The events and the special people in these stories actually were real and so funny and unusual that I had to keep a mental record and some written records in order to pass these adventures on to you, the reader and candidate for many laughs. There will be no certain order of time or events, only stories with titles as I remember them. Names have been changed to protect the guilty and spare the innocent!

Enjoy this book and pass it on to your neighbor. Better yet, keep your copy and buy your friends and family a copy. Let the world know through these pages that old folks do have fun and do have feelings. They even get married again after eighty! They taught me through these twenty-five years that it's never too late in life to venture out, take a dare, have fun, and try something new! Life is full of adventure for those who dare to share it with others! Save your money, young people, so you can live at the Nest someday! Then someone just might write a story about you!

Your author and friend,
Sam Mym

MY MENTOR

Don White became my mentor the first week at the Nest. This man was a gentle giant who stood at about six feet, seven inches—gentle as a lamb but weighed every bit of 250 pounds without his shoes on. He was one of the first residents who moved to the Nest. Don had outlived three wives and had forty grandchildren who came to visit him often. Don had an interesting career. He was the president and CEO of a tie-line zipper company in a smaller town about thirty miles from the capital. After he retired from his business, he took his third wife on a worldwide tour. They were away for about three months when she became very ill and their trip was shortened. He very quickly decided to move into the Nest, along with six other residents who were all charter members.

Every morning, five days a week, he would come to my office door at 9:05 a.m. and greet me with a good-morning smile and a question asking me what I was ready to learn for the day. I guess Don was my trainer and coach because he made sure that I knew every procedure for making coffee in the Piazza and calling bingo and popping the corn for happy hour. He volunteered to help with everything. When one of his many children called him to come to a grandchild's birthday party or graduation party, quite a few times, he would decline due to his commitment to the exercise group or leading the swimming class or even calling bingo on Friday night. He never wanted to let the group down and get a substitute for any of his jobs.

The most shocking thing Don ever did was play an outstanding bride in a womanless wedding. Twenty-five years ago, we had such things as a womanless wedding where the men would dress as women and the women would dress as men. The word *gay* meant fun and happy, and you weren't a crossdresser but just someone having fun. During this fun occasion, Don came out wearing a long black evening gown with a black veil. He was the bride. Following behind him was Dr. Jones dressed in a baby diaper and T-shirt, sucking on a baby bottle and being pulled down the aisle in a little red wagon by Ginnie Mae dressed in a tuxedo; and he was saying to everyone on each side of him, "Are you my daddy? Are you my daddy?" This scene brought the audience down with laughter! The staff was shocked, and Dan's family was aghast at their quiet and reserved father and grandfather playing an Rrated role with such dignity and grace!

The first year at Christmas, Don came into my office with a big grin on his face and an envelope in his hand. He handed it to me and told me that the residents appreciated my hard work. It was a check for $25! I was very surprised, knowing that employees could not accept gifts of any kind from the residents. This was a Christmas bonus given to all employees from the Christmas fund. The money would be divided equally to each employee as a bonus since no tipping or gifts were allowed any other time during the year. This rule was to protect the residents from abuse that might be occurring as residents went through the aging process. There were some residents who had to be protected and guarded carefully by the social workers because they would write checks and give them to the employees just because they could. There were other residents who would respond to the scams that came over the telephone and through the mail. They were stopped and protected as soon as knowledge of this came out. Usually, a resident would come down the hall bragging about the money they had won from the lottery or from the sweepstakes they had entered! Immediate action was taken usually by contacting the family member or the social worker if there was no family member available.

All of the residents at the Nest were very kind and generous. This kindness gave me a feeling of family, so without a doubt, I knew this was my new home forever. Don White had a servant's heart, and we were all blessed by this man's deeds of goodness. He was ninety-one when he passed on to glory land; but a week before he left us, I saw him being wheeled down the hall in a wheelchair carrying a precious, beautiful baby boy! The lady pushing him down the hall was his great-granddaughter.

They stopped me in the hall, and Don proudly smiled and said, "I just wanted you to see my namesake, Don III. He looks just like me, doesn't he?"

I smiled and said, "Yes, he does!"

To this day, I smile when I think of all the times this great man gave time and energy to the residents and staff at the Angel's Nest Nursing Home! His family misses him terribly. So do I!

OUR DEAR JENNA MAE

If there was a very unique and special person to remember at the home, it would definitely be our dear Jenna Mae. Unique and special don't even come close to describing this wonderful, adventuresome lady of eighty-eight years young. Jenna Mae taught me how to throw all my inhibitions out the window and to stop and smell the flowers while catching butterflies! There was not a single thing she could not do or attempt to do, and there was not a single place she had not been or read about.

Jenna's travels took her to Africa on two occasions to hunt wild game. In order to live close by and study the habitat of that particular place and creature that was made by God and would never be harmed by her, she would camp out in tents with the natives around the animal she was studying. The African trips kept her away from us for three to four months at a time. When she would return, we would look forward to seeing all of the artifacts collected as she presented her special program, "Travels with Jenna

Mae," for a full hour or two with slides and vivid details of each experience.

On one of her daring trips, Jenna went whale hunting off the shores of Alaska. She was away for several months, and we all wondered if the trip was too dangerous for her, especially at her age. Jenna proved us wrong again because, when she came home, she had collected whale teeth and some whale lard. For her presentation, she made biscuits that were baked with the whale lard as one of her ingredients and stirred the flour in the bowl with a large whale bone used for a spatula. We thought she had turned into an Eskimo with her unusual but very interesting cooking class. The biscuits were delicious, and there were no complaints about how or why she killed a whale. Some questions we had to keep to ourselves.

The grounds of the ANNH had bluebird houses all around; and our Jenna Mae would keep stats on how many bluebird eggs, how many hatched, when they hatched, and how many houses were cleaned out at the proper time by one maintenance man and Jenna. If a house needed repair, she would get Mr. Kem to fix it in his woodsman shop that was shared by all the men at the home. A collection would be taken up for new houses to be built about every other year or two.

The most fascinating thing our sweet Jenna did was collect dead birds that had fallen prey to a short-lived life from a snake or other predator. She would put the bird in the freezer in a plastic bag, and on Sunday, she would take the bird to her children's Sunday-school class so the children could study the bird and know its habitat. At the end of each school year, during the holidays, Jenna would have her third-grade Sunday-school class name all of the birds they had studied and show the drawings each child had made from her lectures on Sunday mornings about God's beautiful birds that He created for our pleasure. Many of the students could even draw the eggs for each type of bird, and the students would warn the adults to never rob a bird's nest but respect it and save the shells from the eggs after the little baby birds hatched. A great appreciation was developed for all birds, even the little sparrows, just from the children taking an interest in all that our Jenna would bring them each Sunday.

Quilting was another gift she had, and every baby quilt she made by hand was hung on the bulletin board for a week for all to see. Residents would save scraps for Jenna Mae so she could make more quilts. We believe she made about 120 quilts while living at the Angel's Nest Nursing Home! They were all given to mothers in need who could not afford much for the newborn coming! She also gave baby showers for these mothers, and all the ladies in the church and some from the nursing home would make baby sweaters and buy gifts for the newborns! There was quite a mission at the home for the needs of others!

THE RUSSIAN BALLET

The Angel's Nest Nursing Home was a really fun place to work. Two weeks into my employment, we had the Russian ballet visit our home to give us one of their performances. Before heading over to the ballet center, everyone was excited about this event since we had never had a ballet group, much less the Russians coming. When the performers showed up at our little Angel's Nest, I came to realize that we had no room for them to dance because there were thirty of them. What was I to do? The only thing I could do was open up our chapel and let them perform. After all, they had come a long distance, and I wasn't about to disappoint them or our anxious residents! Sister Regina, my boss, was out of town that week. So I really didn't ask permission to move the sacristy and the holy water and the lit candles so that these Russians could run down the aisle in their tutus displaying sashays and ballet leaps and carrying partners on their shoulders to throw to the floor in spins and swan moves! I glanced around the chapel to see if everyone was excited and saw many mouths wide open from excitement as I had imagined.

On Monday morning, I had a visit from Sister Regina!

She was so excited I could hardly understand her dialog, which went something like this: "I realize that you are brand new at this job and you are not familiar with the rules for the chapel. The chapel is a very holy place. We are not allowed to have secular activities in this place. We did not go over this particular rule during orientation, so don't worry, your job is not in jeopardy. But in the future, PLEASE schedule your events for the activity room, unless the event is of a religious nature."

Many of our residents were in shock during the performance, but since the Russians returned everything in its proper place, they were pleased to know that Russians visited the Angel's Nest Nursing Home. This will give them something to talk about for a long, long time.

MS. GRUMPY

There is a short story I will tell you about the grumpy old lady! This lady never had anything good to say about anybody, any place, anytime, or anywhere! She always had a frown on her face, and she always mumbled walking down the hall so low that no one could understand what she was trying to mumble. Thank goodness most residents could not hear what she was saying! If the food was hot, it was too hot. If the food was cold, it was too cold! When we all were in the lobby waiting for the bus to pick us up to go shopping, she complained that the bus was late and never on time. When we went on a day trip, she always had a miserable time and wanted to get back to her apartment before the trip was halfway over. Each month, after a speaker finished his/her program, Ms. Grumpy gave a negative detailed report about not being able to hear the speaker or the speaker talking way too long. Ms. Grumpy frowned so much that her face looked like it was about to crack every time she spoke. We were all surprised each time she came to every activity, never missed a meal, and was always the first one on the bus for a trip to the store or day excursion.

Ms. Grumpy's health became challenging, so her doctor recommended that she move to the assisted-living unit. All the staff helped move her in just a few hours because she didn't have any relatives living and few items in her one-bedroom apartment. The next day, all of the staff members had a sealed envelope in his/her mailbox. Each one of us received the same note which read:

> I want to thank all of the staff here at the Angel's Nest Nursing Home for taking such good care of me during my stay in independent living. Each day, I was met with a smile and sometimes a hug from our activity director and a few of the wonderful housekeepers. The dining staff always gave me an extra helping of butter beans and an extra hot piece of cornbread without me asking. I was always helped on the bus by our dedicated bus driver, and he took my groceries to my room every week after we came home from the grocery store. My deepest thanks goes to the housekeeper staff for giving me an

extra towel and washcloth each week and to the maintenance department for always coming to my room in ten minutes or less when I called weekly complaining about the AC unit in my apartment being too cold or helping me use the remote for my TV that I never could remember how to use. I have always tried to be a simple-minded person, but it was obvious to all that I made life complex. For this, I want to apologize and will try to work on my attitude and daily habits.

Best regards,
Grumpy

The next day, our Ms. Grumpy passed away. We were in *shock*. She is one resident we won't forget!

HELEN STONE, THE VILLAGE ANGEL

Peter and Helen Stone were known as the cutest couple at the Nest. Peter's family had youthful genes, and the men all lived to be over one hundred with no wrinkles. Helen always said that Peter was married to his grandmother. She always wore preppy clothes and only had a few wrinkles, but her warm and loving smile was contagious. Helen walked with God every day all day long. It seemed she had a body halo all around her that glowed, or it could have been angels who stayed with her and guarded her every day. One night, Helen and a few residents drove a car around the lake to stargaze and observe galaxies with a telescope. Helen was so excited she jumped out of the car, forgetting to turn off the engine or putting on the parking brake. The car ran over her feet and legs. Her guardian angels protected her, and no bones were broken. She miraculously walked down the hall the next day singing God's praises and praising the Lord for protecting her frail body from harm!

Peter passed about a year later, and shortly after his passing, Helen met Ned who lived in assisted living. He was a very handsome retired navy man who stood six feet, six inches, to Helen's four feet, ten inches. She would go down to assisted living and read to Ned every day. He fell in love with Helen and called her his sweetheart angel. After fighting and holding back her feelings for several months, Helen fell in love with Ned. They were a very handsome couple. When you saw them walking down the hall, they were always holding hands or hugging each other.

Helen prayed for everyone. She prayed for God to use her granddaughter in a big way. About a year later, her prayers were answered because the granddaughter was called on the mission field to be a foreign missionary. She was stationed across the world in a foreign country for over five years. Helen said after this that you should always be careful what you pray for because the Lord answers prayers in big ways!

One day, when Helen was coming down the hall, I asked her if she would pray for me.

She said, "Honey, what is your greatest desire?"

I told her that I really wanted a soulmate, someone who loved the Lord more than himself, whom my boys would respect, and who would be my best friend and soulmate. She grabbed my hand and prayed for me immediately. One year later, I met my soulmate in church and, eleven months later, became his wife.

Helen outlived her husband, her sweetheart, Ned, and many of her family members. Before her death, she had written several books and had been a Bible teacher for over forty years. She inspired many young women to become Biblical women and to love the Lord more than life! This lady will always be remembered for her strong faith in her Lord, whom she shared with everyone she touched, and for her high standards, the sweet and loving way she had with old and new friends, her shining example of good character and integrity, and her appearance of always looking like a model from *Vogue* magazine. She had it all, and she shared it all with many!

THE MAN WITH
THE PLAN

Frank Low joined our group of residents at a time when the ratio of men to women was one to thirty. He became popular with the ladies and never had to eat alone in the dining room. He loved to go deep-sea fishing and bring his catch back to the home and have a fish fry. At the time of his residency, the home only had about fifty residents, so a fish fry was welcomed and enjoyed. The only requirement Frank had was to let him drink his martinis as he cooked the fish outside and leave him alone while he was cooking the fish.

To try to keep the martinis a secret was not successful! Word got out, and before you could say jackrabbit, Mr. Low had many visitors helping him with his fish fry. One day, I noticed that there were no residents in the dining room waiting for their wonderful lemon fish that was being prepared by Mr. Low. Being concerned that he would not have any takers and he would be cooking too many delicious lemon fish, I quickly ran to the porch outside where he was cooking; and to my surprise, all of the residents were drinking martinis and eating his fish. Everyone was happy, and not one person complained about the food! We had to wheelchair a few of our residents back to their rooms for some odd reason!

After about three months at the home, Mr. Low developed a relationship with two of the lady residents. On Wednesday night, he would have dinner with Lucy. On Tuesdays and Thursdays, he would have lunch with Lacy.

Soon he began having dinner with Lacy, and the word got out that he was really sweet on her.

Each apartment at the home had a kitchen, and some of the ladies would cook for themselves and others. Lucy had been cooking every Wednesday night for Mr. Low. One Wednesday night, when Mr. Low arrived at Lucy's apartment for his regular home-cooked meal, he was greeted at the door with Lucy's teeth and a loud growl! She threw a plate of food at him and told him to take a hike and never show his face at her door again! We were delighted to know the food was on a paper plate! It could have been dangerous!

Shortly after the food tossing, Mr. Low and Lacy were seen during the day at lunch and dinner. They took day trips and discovered new restaurants in the area and brought menus back to me for suggestions. We had an event called Dinner Out once a month to try new dining places, and Mr. Low and Lacy were the chairpersons for the Dinner Out group. They would pick a new place to eat each month, and I would provide the details and sign-up sheet. This worked very well, and our Dinner Out attendance grew to about twenty folks each month.

Mr. Low, being a quiet and humble man, had served as director and chairman of the highest financial group in Washington DC. He never would explain exactly what he did, but we found out from his family that this man controlled all the money that came into the country and passed through our government system in Washington DC for about twelve years! We finally talked him into forming an investment club for some of our residents, and it proved to be very beneficial to those that had a part in the stock market or owned bonds and mutual funds.

PASS THE BASKET

The Hens Are Laying Them Eggs!

Every time the choir would sing a gospel song in choir practice, Mr. Whit would yell out, "Pass the basket. The hens are laying them eggs!"

This man loved gospel music, and he knew just about every song in the old paperback songbooks. He would tell us about his trips to Shiloh Baptist Church to attend the all-day singing and dinner on the ground. He said the folks at Shiloh would sing from 8:00 a.m. 'til the chickens got done on the grills; then around noon, everyone would stop singing and go to eating that barbecue chicken, baked beans, potato salad, and banana pudding and sweet tea made from Mrs. Whit and the other ladies from the church. When everybody was finished stuffing themselves, the singing would start up again and last until about dark thirty!

Mr. Whit had been a funeral director in a little country town, and he was always telling tales about being the last one to let you down and so on and so on. The only problem with his stories was the length. He had all day to rave about things whereas most folks didn't have the time to listen even though the majority of folks were very cordial and polite and some of the men would sit on the loafer's bench in front of the home for hours listening to his tall tales.

Mr. Whit had many gifts to share. He was a basket weaver from a long time ago! The baskets he made out of white oak would keep you spellbound because of their beauty and original design. Mr. Whit would create a new weave and design baskets that would sell for hundreds of dollars at the craft shows, but he only sold them for around $25. If I had to guess, he made at least 250 or more original baskets while at the Angel's Nest.

One day, Mr. Whit decided that he was tired of making those baskets because he was getting older and he wanted to teach others to make the baskets so the art of basket weaving could be preserved. We offered a class in basket weaving. Seven people signed up for the course, including me.

We had to furnish our own material, and to make one basket, we spent about $15. Everyone was so excited.

There was a lovely couple taking the class. They were not married, but the friendship between them was most unusual and strong. Fred and Eunice argued most of the time but seemed to have a bond between them. Fred lost his wife about four months before Eunice moved into the home. He was very lonely and needed a companion friend. Eunice fit the bill, and they ate their lunch and dinner meals together. Some nights, they would come down to the activity room and watch a ball game together. Fred was not allowed into Eunice's apartment because she was a very old-fashioned lady who believed in never letting an unmarried man into a single lady's home. He never entered her front door, but they created a stronger bond when they began making those white-oak baskets.

Mr. Whit told me that Fred and Eunice argued so much that it was useless for them to even take the basket-weaving class. With a lot of patience, the couple stayed and eventually caught on to the art of basket weaving. As a matter of fact, the two of them made over four hundred original baskets and sold almost all of them to the public and even had articles published about them in the *Southern Living* magazine. They shocked Mr. Whit and the world with their wonderful and amazing determination to be basket weavers!

GEORGE STAUER, OUR SNOWBIRD

The news of a single-again man from Florida coming to live with us spread fast. The ladies began to inquire at the front desk about his arrival, and each week, the eligible ladies would gather at the mailboxes and discuss who would ask him to lunch first. Finally, the day came, and George stepped out of the taxi followed by a moving van. Our welcome committee was there to greet him, and of the five committee members, two of them were single ladies who had prepared to take George to lunch. He looked like a tanned Greek god who carried a smile and a greeting that melted these two on the spot.

"Hello, beautiful ladies. You two look ravishing," said he.

His reputation spread like wildfire, and all of the ladies wanted to be complimented by this handsome snowbird.

It seemed rather strange that George never would ask any of the ladies to lunch. Each day, when he came down toward the dining room, there would be one of the catch-him-if-you-can girls waiting to grab his arm and escort him into the dining area. This seemed to please him for a few weeks, but after some cross words from a few of the candidates for marriage came in awkward moments of embarrassment for him, he came to me for help. He did not want to hurt anyone's feelings, but George was a one-woman man. He cared for his loving wife for over twelve years when she came down with cancer. He retired from his lucrative job and stayed by her side, loving her and caring for her. The thought of marrying another woman made him ill, just thinking about it. He was truly a gentleman and a scholar who made everyone feel special, and his com-pliments were sincere to each person he greeted whether it was the housekeeper or the financial officer. He was pleas-ant and caring to everyone.

We plotted and planned for a few weeks, and then the idea hit hard. I had a friend that was young and drop-dead gorgeous. She had been single now for at least ten years and was not dating anyone at present. Bonnie came to the home one day and met George. He was smitten but tried not to show it. This lady was an angel and looked heavenly to him. She was to have lunch with George that day so the ladies at the home would "back off." When they came into the dining room, everyone froze and stared at the dashing couple. George was at least twelve to fifteen years older than Bonnie, but their personalities were matched to perfection! They laughed and made eye contact that was giving out the message of cupid working overtime!

Gossip groups began to spread the word that these two lovebirds were going to get married for sure or live in sin because they were inseparable. Bonnie took George out to eat, and they even began painting in oils together. Day trips to a site for painting were common for them. George even went to church with Bonnie and donated a large sum of money to the church-building fund and the missionary fund. He was a very wealthy man, and Bonnie had plenty of money as well. Excursions to Europe and Spain came about five months after they began seeing each other. George was happy, and Bonnie was content. They were very comforting to one another. Bonnie had lost her husband in a terrible accident about ten years ago, and she never got the spark back in her eyes until George.

The ladies at the home forgave him for his abandonment of them because, about three months after George arrived, the cupid fairy brought three more men to the home. Each one was different but available. Lunches became pleasant again for the catch-him-if-you-can girls, and all was well at the sweet Angel's Nest Nursing Home.

MY THORN IN THE
FLESH, CHRIS

My first thorn in the flesh was Mrs. Chris Shavers, but only for a little while. Several events brought us to a much better relationship, but it took some work on both sides. When I met this lady, who was one of my bubbling residents, she informed me of being totally or legally blind. She hid it well. When a new resident came to the Nest, Chris would give them a tour and a brief orientation, take them to lunch, and introduce them to the family of residents. This was very helpful to the staff and to Chris because she had a sense of belonging. The staff even gave her a badge that she proudly wore every day that said "ambassador."

Every afternoon before I left the office, I would make a recording of the activities for the next day. The residents would call to hear these announcements. Chris, being legally blind, could not read the bulletin board. She depended on the recording announcements to get her through the day and to get me riled up. It never failed. Each day, about 9:00

a.m., Chris would give me a call and let me know that I had left off this or had forgotten that. One day, she got so mad she came by the office to let me have it. She was going to have me fired because I never once did the announcements correctly. I apologized to her for my negligence and asked her to please teach me how to properly do the morning announcements.

She taught me a lot that day. Her daily critiques helped me become a better activity director for all of the residents. Each morning, I would greet Chris when I saw her in the hall with "Morning, Coach"; and she would respond with "Good morning, student of mine" with a smile!

The following year, we took Chris to the Senior Olympics, which was held at a junior college close by. One of the larger banks sponsored this yearly event, which included senior adults statewide who would come and enter over fifty events designed for seniors. Some of the events included running, badminton, tennis, baseball throw, football throw, croquet, basketball, and shuffleboard. Chris was very excited to be chosen as part of the Angel's Nest Nursing Home Senior Olympic team! In her division, which was eighty to eighty-five years of age, she won a gold medal in the softball throw! We had over ten residents who won gold medals that year! The day we brought the gold medalists back to the Nest, there was a huge celebration in the dining room just for these winners! All ten gold-medal winners paraded around the dining room, waving their medals as the residents applauded and cheered each one with a standing ovation! This was one of the happiest days for our champion Chris as well as the other nine champions! Chris hung her gold medal on the bulletin board along with a picture from the Olympics with her proudly receiving the award! As new residents would come to the Nest, Chris would take them by the bulletin board and show them her medal, adding details and promoting the Senior Olympic events!

One day, Chris was unable to live in independent living, so she had to move to assisted living where she was greeted by others who had gone before her. The residents and nurses made her feel very loved and special. She came by my office as she was moving and told me to feel free to give her a call at any time if I needed help and to please come and visit her often—which I did!

MY SECOND THORN IN THE FLESH, MILLIE

Millie Ray was married to Ernie Ray, who was one of the kindest men I had ever met! Ernie was frail yet strong in character with integrity and humility along with kindness that he shared with everyone. Millie was his caregiver and devoted wife. Ernie loved to laugh while Millie never cracked a smile.

Every Thursday, one of the residents would lead a Bible study. Helen Stone, an angel who is mentioned in the book, was teaching at least twice a month. Millie would sit in the back of the room with a teacher's guide, taking notes to critique Helen after each class was over. One week, Helen came to me, looking very discouraged. She told me that Millie would stare at her during the Bible-study class and write notes, which would be read to her in criticism after each session. Helen wanted to scream at her but did not know what to do, knowing that a Christian Bible teacher had to have patience and love for her fellow believers. She was asking for my advice, so I politely told her that she was God's messenger and not Millie's pincushion. We laughed!

The bulletin board was my responsibility. Keeping the announcements current of activities and special events was not an easy task. I never had many creative ideas for the board, and it wasn't my favorite thing to do. So very often, I made mistakes. Millie would call my attention to these mistakes by sending me a note or a personal phone call. For Millie, this was joyful and challenging; but for me, it was an irritation that would soon simmer. After all, I was working for the residents; they were not working for me. Every time we had an outside speaker, which was quite often, Millie would ask if I had written a thank-you note to the speaker. Of course, she would always ask me this the day after we had a special speaker, so I was always replying, "Not yet." One day, I asked Millie if she would take on this task since she was so good at writing notes. She agreed to do so, and I began to see and understand Millie a little better. I think she just wanted me to ask her for help, which she gave willingly at any request.

I never will forget the party we had after a fashion show. We had hired a caterer for this event because some very important people had been invited—the mayor, the city alderman, and the sheriff, who were all ladies. The caterer told me to direct the line of people in another direction so that they could pick up their food first and their drinks last. Millie was leading the group first in line but going in the opposite direction. I asked Millie to please redirect the line just as the caterer had requested. A direct order from me to Millie was not kosher. She jumped back and told me in no uncertain terms that she was not going in another direction other than her apartment. She left abruptly, marching out of the room toward the elevators. Her pot was boiling over, and everyone knew it. I did not show panic on the outside, but on the inside, my mind was rushing and my prayer was "Lord, now what?" He answered my prayer with this thought: take her a plate. I immediately prepared her a plate and flew to her apartment. After one knock on her door, Millie opened the door with her gown on and her hair in hairpins. She was going to bed without her supper. I apologized to Millie for not getting a plate of food and handed her one. The iceberg around her body melted when a smile came on her face that shocked me and almost took my breath away. She told me I should not have left the party to bring her a plate, but she thanked me over and over again. The next morning, there was a thank-you note on my desk in script with no red marks. That event was the turning point for both of us. We became friends that night, and I did not receive another critique verbally or in writing ever again from Millie!

43

THE MAN WHO
KILLED THE GOOSE
AT THE LAKE

There was a beautiful lake at the home that everybody enjoyed from time to time by fishing in it, viewing it from the balconies, or just walking around it during fair weather. The powers that be decided to spend some money on a sidewalk that went all around the lake so more residents and employees could enjoy the outdoors and get more exercise. As expected, many folks got out of their apartments and walked around the body of water viewing the fish, geese, ducks, and egrets! Benches were placed at certain spots by trees so the not-so-in-shape residents could rest along their journey. Even the residents in wheelchairs were able to be pushed around the lovely water, and employees were challenged to walk during their lunch breaks to get in shape for the longevity of life.

Things were going very smoothly; and the community was happy and feeling tolerably well when, all of a sudden, there was a great tragedy! Mr. Frank was taking his morning stroll before breakfast, which he normally did every day except Sunday, around the lake. The geese were heavily populating the area and becoming a nuisance due to the goose poop they were leaving on the sidewalk. Some of the residents refused to walk on the path until the goose poop was cleared away by maintenance or administration. Anyway, back to Mr. Frank. He was minding his own business and admiring the beautiful day when a male goose began to run toward him. Mr. Frank carried a big walking stick on his journeys, but today he had forgotten to bring it along. The goose jumped toward Mr. Frank, and to preserve his life to the fullest, Mr. Frank grabbed the goose around the neck! It was the goose or Mr. Frank to survive! With much energy and in a state of panic, Mr. Frank choked the goose and dropped him to the ground. The goose was dead. Mr. Frank was terrified! When he reached the other side of the lake, a crowd was there to greet him with applause and hugs for killing the mean goose who had chased many folks off of their walking paths. Mr. Frank did not receive the crowd in a warm fashion. He took off to his apartment with great speed and was reported to have left the premises to never return, carrying two suitcases and his laptop!

A GREAT SOUTHERN
LADY

Being situated in the South has given the home a wonderful group of Southern ladies. One of them in particular is a precious resident whom we will call Jeanette. This lady had fifty grandchildren that she was very proud of to the point of posting her family tree on the bulletin board! Everyone would come by and read her family tree with comments that were very favorable. Every holiday, like Christmas and Easter, all of her children and grandchildren would come to see her; and she would be showing them off one by one and telling stories about each child and grandchild.

Jeanette would tell us many stories about her niece Dale Evans, who was married to Roy Rogers. Twice a year, Jeanette and Dale would get together at the home, or Jeanette would travel to see Dale at her home. She would bring back pictures of them as well as Roy Rogers and his famous horse, Trigger! She also had many movies with Dale and Roy, and she shared them with all of us. There were many autographed photos of Dale, Roy, and her children that were seen in Jeanette's apartment. We all thought that Jeanette was a celebrity because of her beautiful and gentle demeanor. She was always happy and always smiling, and she always had a compliment for anyone that she was talking to. Many times, she would invite residents to her apartment for afternoon tea and cookies, all of which she made herself. Jeanette even wrote a cookbook with her famous recipes that she had collected from her mother, her grandmother, her greatgrandmother, and her niece Dale Evans. The book was published, and most of the residents purchased this cookbook. Jeanette even autographed each cookbook with a personal message that was warm and friendly. When a resident was sick or if they had been in the hospital and had returned to their home, Jeanette would always cook some banana bread or lemon meringue pie or coconut cake and take it to them. She was a goodwill ambassador who gave the village a beautiful reputation for being warm, hospitable, and inviting. When a new resident would come to the home, Jeanette would greet them in the lobby and give them a special tour of the activity center, the dining room, the exercise room, and the library; and she would walk them around the lake, showing them the best fishing spots. This dear lady lived a full and abundant life, and her legacy was one of a true Southern lady who loved everyone and made them feel special.

DR. NATHANIEL
QUENTIN'S LEGACY

We were very fortunate to have Dr. Nathaniel Quentin. He came to us from New York with very important credentials. He was a doctor of literature and a librarian of forty years.

At least once a week, Dr. Quentin would come to my office and share many stories about his journeys and adventures in New York. This man was very intelligent, and he was not embarrassed to tell everyone and share with everyone about his knowledge. Each week, the good doctor would have an event in the activity room that we labeled an enrichment class.

We began calling this event Nat's Video, which led to his nickname, Nat. He liked his new name, and he said it made him feel normal, like one of the fellow residents.

The videos were famous operas, musicals, old movie classics, documentaries, and historical events. This wonderful weekly event made Nat very popular among the residents, and he was well respected by all. His confidence level soared to new heights, and Nat began to bring outside speakers to enlighten us even further.

There were presidents of colleges, doctors, some criminal defense lawyers, and a few politicians, including the retired governor from New York! We were learning in unfamiliar worlds and loving all of it.

Dr. Quentin loved to travel and drive himself everywhere. This man was eighty-five years young and wore reading glasses (to hear him tell it) that were about one-half inch thick. He used a cane and should have been using a rollator, but his pride would never hear of it. He did not come to my office for about three consecutive days, so being concerned, I went to the village nurse to ask if he had taken ill. She had not seen him in weeks, so my curiosity led me to the morning clerk, who checked on the rolls. He was in Texas attending a computer programming seminar.

On one beautiful morning, Nat came running into the office and wanted to talk for at least one hour. I always made time for Dr. Quentin because he had wonderful ideas and I loved to pick his brain! Computers were not popular with our residents, and no one knew how to use them. All of the employees had gone to computer class in order to operate the computer in each office. Dr. Nathaniel Quentin wanted to have a computer workshop and invite all of the residents. We organized this event for a Saturday, including lunch! There were thirty-two attendees!

Following this workshop, at least ten of the residents purchased computers, and we chose a resident to become the computer chairman. We named the group the "Computer Club," and this started a chain of events, putting this little nursing home far above others with innovative and progressive actions! Needless to say, our Dr. Nathaniel Quentin was featured in the local newspaper as a man of progression and expertise! Our Nat left this world with a wonderful legacy of making the Angel's Nest Nursing Home a fun and smart place to be! We will always be grateful to our friend Nat and carry his memories with us along with our skills in computer!

THE NAKED LADY

There are many stories to tell about residents in a retirement home, but this one takes the prize. This lady, whom we will call Mrs. West to protect her from her guilt, was a lady that had no modesty, no inhibitions, no embarrassing moments, and no apologies for any words or jokes that came out of her mouth. Mrs. West was a retired college literature professor who had written several books and plays while teaching at a very liberal university in the northern part of the country. We will just leave it there.

When she moved into our calm and quiet home, the entire organizational staff member teams began to buzz about this most unusual lady. The conversations were not gossip sessions at coffee breaks but rather surprise events that shocked the group, including any men present. Each day or two, someone would have another "shocking" story to tell.

Not very far into her first month of residency, Mrs. West began to meander down to the morning coffee group of residents so that she could make herself known to the group and possibly find some companionship by making new friends, or so we believe. She came into the room making a grand entrance wearing a snug bright-orange minidress draped with a bronze rooster-feather shoulder wrap, wearing four-inch heels, and carrying a leather clutch bag that held her Sweet'N Low French vanilla creamer for her coffee.

Everyone stopped their conversations and began to stare at this most unusual resident. She smiled and thanked them for their undivided attention and began to tell her first joke that led to many during her stay at the Angel's Nest Nursing Home! To give the joke an R-rating would not be fair. It was rated XX, and folks talked about her and her grand entrance for many days. She would smile, sip her coffee, and let others carry on snippets of conversation; then she would engage them in some of her wild tales from the past at "her" university. This went on for quite a while because she would only come down on Wednesday mornings, giving the residents six more days to ponder and share her wild and most unique stories with others. Mrs. West was a board member at the largest bank in town. So she had one of the bank officers bring donuts every Wednesday to the coffee klatch, and the group began to increase in numbers. One Wednesday morning, I counted at least forty residents having coffee and donuts listening to Mrs. West tell her joke for the week!

Each day at ANNH (Angel's Nest Nursing Home) was usually cool and calm except for the excitement which Mrs. West brought to the maintenance department one day around 10:00 a.m. She called to place a work order for maintenance, asking them to please come to her apartment and fix her microwave so she could heat her tea. One of the men promptly came to her door about fifteen minutes after the call had been made. He knocked on her apartment door and heard a voice saying to please come in. As he opened the door, he saw a naked lady on the couch reading a book, and he slammed the door! Shocked and disturbed, he went back to the maintenance office to report the incident. The director called Mrs. West and asked her to please put on some clothes so the men could come and fix her micro-wave. She explained in a sharp voice that she never wore clothes in her apartment and she was insulted that any-one would take offense to her beautiful body! The director explained that there was no offense taken and also tried to explain that, in the South, most ladies stayed clothed while workers worked. Mrs. West slammed the phone down, and about two days later, she came into the administrator's office with a complaint. The administrator was aware of the situation and told her that the staff would not be able to satisfy her requests unless she was fully clothed or away from her apartment at the time of working on any request. She agreed to always be away from her apartment while the rude men carried on their labors.

This story stayed in the buzz for a long time. Mrs. West continued to make her grand entrances on Wednesdays to the large coffee klatch group; and she passed away years later, leaving a large sum of money to the activity department to spend on coffee, coffee makers, refreshments, and donuts.

THE ATOM BOMB

During my wonderful years at the home, I met some very incredible and rare folks. One of those rare beings was Mr. Jack Hayes. This man would walk down the hall with his head down and travel at a most unusual walking speed for his age of eighty-five. If you spoke to him with a "Good morning," he would nod his head and keep walking. When he and his lovely bride would come down for dinner each evening, his wife, Ethel, would carry on a conversation with the other residents at the dinner table while Mr. Jack ate his meal in silence. Jack and Ethel would walk back down the hall to their apartment smiling at each other and carrying on a busy conversation between the two of them. If someone passed by, they would stop talking, nod at the person, then continue on their merry way.

One morning, I went into the exercise room to check out all of the equipment, which I did each month to be sure all of the bicycles, treadmills, rowing machines and the Bowflex were in working order. To my surprise, Mr. Jack Hayes was riding on one of the Airdyne bikes. The tread-mill was parallel to the Airdyne, so I jumped on the tread-mill and began to walk at a slow pace. After about three minutes, Mr. Jack glanced my way, so I politely said good morning to him. He gave me a reply that it was a good morning. My curiosity was stirred, so we began a conversation with the type of work he was involved in before he and Mrs. Ethel moved to the home. The time slipped by, and after about forty-five minutes of deep conversation, I asked Mr. Jack if he would be our very first storyteller and come to the activity room at his convenience to tell his remark-able story. He smiled and said he would be delighted. I immediately began planning the next month's activities to include the storyteller, Mr. Jack Hayes. When the calendar for the month was placed in everyone's mailbox, the buzz began! At least twenty folks came into my office in amaze-ment that Mr. Jack would be talking to a group of resi-dents for thirty minutes telling a story. They didn't think he could talk. He had never said a word to any of them, and for this man to put himself at the mercy of the residents was a shock in mild terms!

The day finally came for our first storyteller series. Each month, a resident would be selected to tell a story about their past or about anything worthy of a group of people listening to and being held captive for thirty min-utes. The room was full, and there were not any seats left.

It was about ten minutes before Jack was to speak. He had not come into the room, so I was a bit concerned that he had backed out possibly. So very casually, I slipped out of the activity room and began looking for Mr. Jack. Passing the mailboxes and to the left was our library. Mr. Jack was sitting in the red chair by the shelves of books, just inside the door of the library. In his hand was a glass half full of Scotch whisky. He was slowly sipping this drink when I walked in. I calmly asked if he was ready to tell his story.

His reply went like this, "I'll tell my story if you won't tell Mrs. Ethel about this," as he held up the glass.

"You have my word on that" was my reply.

In what seemed to be one smooth motion, he drank the remaining scotch, stood up, grabbed his notes, and escorted me back into the activity room. The crowd began to applaud as we entered the room. As I introduced Mr. Hayes, you could hear a pin drop because the audience was already spellbound. He began speaking with a calmness that mesmerized all of us, and we were paralyzed as he began to tell us about the secret city of Oak Ridge that consisted of sixty thousand acres nestled in the ridges of East Tennessee. This city was cloaked in secrecy during WWII where tens of thousands of people flocked to during the war helping to build the world's first atomic bomb. Jack told us about his role in this strategic task and how all the silver was taken from the United States Treasury Department and used to make this bomb. He said that it was all returned except for one-tenth of an ounce. His wife, Ethel, was the secretary for this mission; and she had secrets that could not be revealed even to him. This man was so intelligent and so precise in his description of making the atomic bomb that we were stricken with shock and disbelief for over an hour. He finally concluded with a joke about the feds, and we laughed and applauded with a standing ovation!

CONFESSIONS GOOD FOR THE SOUL

My office was down the hall near our chapel and right next to the sacristy, which was a small room where all of the pastors and priests would come to prepare for mass or worship services. The chapel was a beautiful place for all denominations and nondenominations to come in and worship. As I described in earlier chapters, all of the walls were covered in stained-glass Bible story creations that were made and donated by a famous artist and sculptor. There were large stained-glass windows that measured four feet by four feet, and then there were smaller stained-glass windows that measured ten inches by ten inches. Each window was designed from a specific verse in the Bible or a story from the Bible. Two sides of the chapel had outside walls, and the entrance was from the hallway next to my office. It was a beautiful place with high ceilings and seats for about seventy-five to eighty folks.

When guests came for a tour of the facility, I would bring them to the chapel; and as they gazed at the beautiful stained-glass windows, the scheduled use of the chapel would be repeated: Monday for Methodists, Tuesday for Baptists, Wednesday for Episcopals, Thursday for Presbyterians, Friday for all, and Monday through Friday at 8:30 a.m. for Catholic Mass. This little chapel had a piano and an organ with a beautiful altar. Just being inside gave you a feeling of peace.

When it was time for the Catholics to have confession, which was about two times a year, they would need to use my office; and I would find myself going to other areas to visit or conduct an activity. One of the priests loved to "carry on" with me, and he was quite the prankster. When confessions were over, I would find Father Fran the next day and tell him it took at least four hours to wash all those sins off my walls. He would laugh and make an apology for the inconvenience. This schedule went on for several years, and we had fun joking with each other. He was an Irish Catholic who really believed in the luck of the Irish, and I was a foot-washing, hard-shell Baptist who sang those good ole gospel hymns every chance a piano was close by.

Father Fran was transferred to another town about two hours away, so we had a farewell party for him. We all made him dance with us even though he had two left feet, and all of the nurses put on deep-red lipstick and kissed his bald head as he left us that day. We were all very sad to see him go, and as I walked to my office with tears, they soon turned to laughter! Father Fran had left the maid's cart with a wet mop and bucket in the middle of my office with a note: "I washed them all off for you this time. Please keep this office clean for me until I come back again." He was missed by us all!

THE SISTERS
GO FISHING

To be able to work with sisters of the faith was incredible! They swore an oath of poverty and were always helping others with prayers and giving communion to those who were not able to attend mass, listened to constant complaints about the nursing-home food, and led memorial services when others failed to show up. They could have been hurting all over with arthritis or gout, but no complaining ever came out of their mouths. (It might have been different when they went home to the convent to relax after eight to ten hours of hard work at the nursing home.)

My husband and I had a pontoon boat on a beautiful lake and decided to take the sisters on a fishing outing so they could let go and have fun! I told them to wear comfortable clothes and to let me know what their favorite drinks were. I wanted to surprise them with some fun, food, and good ale or wine or beer. The selections varied; and one cooler contained red wine, light beer, sarsaparilla,

Diet Coke, Sprite, water, and Kentucky bourbon. There were eight sisters attending the outing, with four wearing their full habits, two wearing pants and comfortable blouses, and two wearing long skirts and caps to block the sun. Nothing stopped any of them from having a fun time!

We began our day of fun around 3:00 p.m. Our pontoon had a cover, so the sun was not a problem. Only four of the sisters wanted to fish while the others enjoyed the wind, waves, and beautiful surroundings. Sister Mary Rose had been raised on a farm, so she helped us teach the others how to cast the rod into the water and troll. What fun it was to see each of them catch a fish or two! Each time, we would all yell and scream even if the fish was only the size of a minnow. Sister Mary Rose caught a five-pound bass, and we had to grab her before she jumped off the back of the pontoon trying to reel that big boy in! (We froze him for a future fish fry.)

Around 6:00 p.m., we decided to pull our fishing poles in and just ride around the lake to see all of the beautiful homes and boathouses that were built there. It was about the first week in October, and the temperature was just perfect.

As the boat passed each homeplace, the sisters would stand and wave at any folks who were in their yards or standing on their private piers and yell, "God bless you!"

The replies were always "And also you!"

The sun was setting rather quickly for us, and little did we realize that it was 8:00 p.m. and the moon was rising. We were in the middle of this lake without any lights except the small light on the front and the back of our pontoon boat. I remembered having a flashlight in the storage bin, so with it and eight sisters praying for guidance, we made it back to our pier without a single incident. With all of the sisters having the vow of moderation, my husband and I had a cooler full of mixed drinks that we saved for another fun day with our dear sister friends! Several weeks after our fishing fun day, we were asked by several of our friends from the lake if we were having a Halloween party early and why didn't they get invited.

CROQUET, ANYONE?

The grounds at the nursing home were never level, so outside events were very limited. One of the residents wanted to organize a croquet team, but we could never find a level place to play. There was a small area between our chapel and the main hall, which had some trees and a sidewalk on two sides. Two sides were glassed in with large windows, so the folks could look out onto the lovely yard as they walked to the chapel or into the activity room or dining room.

We decided to put the court there so residents could play and others could view the games from inside. Small tables and chairs were placed on the two sidewalks for players and spectators. It was a cozy area of play, nothing like a regulation field, but the atmosphere was perfect for short games and a social gathering at the same time!

The players wore white, and the official drink was the Pimm's Cup, which we allowed to be made with lemonade to make the drink tasty and the players sober throughout the games. Teams were formed, and the charter members totaled sixty-five.

The news spread far and wide about our official croquet club, and the newspaper was thrilled to come and
take pictures of the charter members for the front page
of the paper! Family members attended and cheered for
their loved ones whenever we had the croquet extravaganza
twice a year because elaborate food was served to all who
attended the games. During the extravaganzas, there would
be music from local bands or small combos. Excitement
swept the town, and news of this senior adult croquet club
spread for miles. The club members who actually played
each week totaled around twenty-four on a good day while
the other charter members attended the games to share in
the refreshments and hear the entertainment. Most of our
folks had a wonderful time either playing or socializing
among their neighbors.

As the home grew in size, so did the croquet club. The
new activity room held two hundred folks, and the Good
Things Better Committee decided that a new croquet field
was imperative as well as a seven-hole putting green and a
beautiful veranda overlooking the game areas. The board
of directors gave their approval for the new additions; and
in just a short time, we had a beautiful veranda overlooking our lake, adorned with the croquet and golf. Activities
buzzed as the games were played, and even bands came
to add music to the festivities. The food was often served

outside on many occasions when there were games being played. All of the club members wore white because preserving the game was of the utmost importance!

Croquet became a very competitive sport, and word spread all over the South. The Angel's Nest Nursing Home had made the big leagues, and there were teams coming in from far and wide to play this very competitive group of "old folks wearing white." There weren't many victories for the old folks, but there were many occasions for picture taking and trophies for grand sportsmanship. The wickets that were permanently placed on the court were from Canada and made the headlines in the local paper: "ONLY ONE-EIGHTH INCH FOR THE BALL TO PASS THROUGH THE WICKET," and these old folks could master the task! No yard croquet for them. No! No! Competition at its finest!

THE SURPRISE
BETROTHAL

John was an oilman who came to live with us when he was in his early eighties and was a most wealthy man indeed. He would take the residents on field trips and treat them all to lunch. One day, he gave a party for the Angel's Nest Nursing Home and invited the mayor and the police chief as guests.

No expense was spared that day. Hors d'oeuvres and champagne were plentiful, and the entertainment was a five-piece band from another town. We all decided that his party was the biggest and finest event of the year. John never bragged about his money; he just spent it—mostly on others. This made him extremely happy, so we never complained. He never stopped giving of himself or his money for very extravagant and fun events.

The ladies didn't seem to flock to him. But he always had a dinner date, and he was always carrying a lady out to a fine restaurant on many occasions. Each time, he would be with a different lady, and all of the ladies bragged on his manners and gentleman ways. Several afternoons, John would invite a lady friend over for a glass of wine and snack foods from international and foreign places where he had traveled while in the oil business.

One day, our vivacious resident Libby Teaver came to the beauty salon with a four-karat engagement ring on her left hand. She made sure everyone saw her magnificent and unique ring that carried sapphires and diamonds around the four-karat center diamond. All of the ladies were shocked and in awe when Libby told them she was going to marry John the oilman. The shock came because Libby was very wealthy and had a summer home in the mountains. To top that off, she was never seen with John at the village or anywhere else for that matter.

Two weeks passed, and the married couple made a grand entrance into the dining room. The entire resident population applauded as they entered the room, and one of the men asked them how they pulled it off without anyone knowing. Libby replied that she had always wanted to marry a man who had more money than she and one that knew about fine dining. John replied that he had his eyes on Libby for quite some while and that it took him a year of courting her in secret to get a yes for marriage. One of the ladies asked how they did it because no one had a clue that they were a couple. John replied that, while everyone was going to bed by 7:00 p.m., he and Libby were painting the town red. The courtship lasted one year in secret, and the wedding was attended by the preacher only!

WEDDING BELLS

The Angel's Nest Nursing Home had a chapel. It was a beautiful place to worship. On Monday, for Methodists; Tuesday, for Baptists; Wednesday, for Episcopals; Thursday, for Presbyterians; Friday, for anybody; and Monday through Friday at 8:30 a.m., Mass for the Catholics. The little chapel was full of beautiful handmade stained-glass windows that had a scripture verse or Bible story attached to them in some way. The residents' families were allowed to have a memorial service in the chapel for their loved one's passing but no funerals. One lady wanted to be cremated and her ashes brought in for a memorial service, but that was not permitted. One bouquet of flowers was permitted in front of the altar but no wreaths on stands or potted plants. The establishment wanted to keep the home lively and not overkill with funerals all the time, so the memorial service was established for closure. So family members and residents had the chance to say goodbye to the passing resident in a respectful way.

Over a ten-year period, there were five weddings in the little chapel. I will attempt to describe cupid's journey that led to each wedding occasion.

Barbara Pearson came to us from the country. She was a farm girl and had about five hundred acres of rich farmland that would be given to her children at her death. She came to the home because, at seventy-two years of age, she wanted more out of life. She wanted to find a new husband since her beloved had passed away the year before she came. It was no secret to everyone that her goal was to catch a man! Barbara joined every activity that the Angel's Nest could offer. Her energy was contagious. She recruited as many men to join the choir and croquet as possible. Every day, she would invite a man to eat lunch with her; and because she could still drive, she would take a man out to dinner every day that one would accept her offer of a free meal. This lady had money, and everybody knew it! She was also a hard-shell Baptist, and everybody knew it.

One day, Joe came to the home! When Barbara saw him, she immediately fell in love! She pampered him, gave him gifts, and took him to dinner, lunch, and breakfast. Joe was a shy man, and he did not know how to take this aggressive lady and her gifts! He was a Catholic who loved to take a nip of alcohol on occasion. Barbara was a teetotaler who never touched the stuff but swore on a stack of Bibles that she would accept his little nip at dinner if he would go out with her the next day. He agreed to this arrangement, and the fussing stopped. Joe joined the choir, and before long, everyone was talking about the romance of Barbara and Joe. Barbara would sit across the room in the alto section staring at Joe, who sat with the men across the room in the bass section. Immediately after choir, she would grab Joe by the hand, and off they would go on another adventure! Several months passed, and the announcement came: a wedding in the chapel. Everyone was invited. The reception would be in the activity room immediately following the ceremony. A Baptist preacher and a Catholic priest married Joe and Barbara, and at the reception, there were two punch tables: one with alcohol and one without. Barbara said that she was one happy Baptist Catholic!

The next wedding came about a year later. Coleen was a sweet little lady who came to the home still mourning the death of her late husband. She joined the line dancers to keep her mind and body busy. Workout mode was her theme to keep her mind occupied and her moods on a positive swing. Six months passed by fairly quickly for her, and then a nice-looking gentleman came to the home. Bob was tall, handsome, well dressed, and single again. His wife had passed several years back, and he had retired and traveled for a few years before settling at the Angel's Nest.

Bob quickly fit in with all of the residents and joined the line-dancing group. He did not know any of the steps and needed some help catching up. Coleen volunteered to help him after class with some private coaching. He agreed to this offer, and after each line-dancing class, Coleen and Bob would stay in the activity room to dance. The dancing led to long conversations that led to walks around the campus that led to lunch dates that led to dinner dates that led to a visit to my office one fine day. This couple was concerned about the gossip that was buzzing around them every time they walked the halls. My reply to the gossip was simple: "Just get married, and it will stop." Two weeks later, they were married in the chapel with only family and close friends present. The gossip stopped.

In the spring of the next year, we had a dance in the dining room. All the ladies were dressed in their Sunday dresses, and the men wore coats and ties. A quartet symphony ensemble came to play for this fancy and festive affair. Carlene and Bill danced every dance together. He would not dance with anyone else. This made all the ladies jealous because the ratio of men to ladies was still around two to thirty, and that made most of the ladies sitting throughout the night without a dance partner. We began seeing Carlene and Bill together at lunch, and when there was a speaker or outside group performing, they would sit together. Bill was the resident association president, and he carried a lot of clout around, being a retired lawyer. If anything was to be done or changes were to be made, folks would come to Bill for the answers or solutions to all of their problems, or so it seemed.

The home needed a new activity building. The present one was so small that it only held sixty folks at a time, and the home was growing very fast. Plans had been drawn for a new building, but nothing was happening. Bill decided to get a petition and have every resident sign it. Carlene was his superstar. She would stand at the dining room door at every meal, and the residents would hear her plea and sign the petition. In about two weeks, she and Bill had every signature on the petition, about 185 at the time. Bill took the petition to the higher powers, and within a year, the new activity center was built. During this process, Carlene and Bill had gotten very close and did nothing without the other present. One day, the couple was coming down the hall, and Bill fainted. Carlene screamed for help! The nurse called the ambulance, and they arrived in ten minutes to take Bill to the hospital.

Carlene wanted to ride with him. The attendant said that only family members could ride in the ambulance. Carlene flashed a wedding band in the attendant's face and held Bill's hand up to see a matching wedding band. She proudly said that she was his wife as of the day before and that she was riding with her husband to the emergency room! The secret was out, and the happy couple moved into the same apartment shortly after Bill recovered!

The rumors were running all over the home that a tall man from Mexico was coming to live at the Angel's Nest! The ladies would go to the front desk and ask every day if he had arrived. Shortly after the news, he did arrive. Tom was a dashing and tall man with a huge smile and a sparkling personality. He never met a stranger, and the ladies surrounded him with smiles and their best behavior. A group of the single ladies would congregate at the mailboxes, waiting for him to check his mail. He would always have a smile and pleasant conversation for them as he entered the hall or the dining room. The men didn't have much to say because the ladies never gave him a chance to venture over to the men at any one time. Tom was asked each week to have lunch or dinner with a lady one day, then a different lady the next. He loved all of the attention he was getting and would come into my office to chat and discuss his status.

Tom was getting over the death of his beloved wife who had passed only a few short months before, and he was not interested in getting married or even having a serious relationship with a woman. He was quite the gentleman and did not want to hurt anyone's feelings, so he continued lunches and dinners to have a conversation with the ladies, hoping it would ease his broken heart for his beloved late wife. He had a master's in music and taught music history at a university in the States until he retired and moved to Mexico, where he met his beautiful wife, Melanie. Tom knew there would never be anyone to take her place and no one would ever match her beautiful looks and personality. After Tom had lived at the home for about six months, a lady moved into the Angel's Nest, and all of the men stopped in their tracks when she came into the room. Lydia was a tall, blonde, beautiful, and elegant lady who made the room radiate when she entered. The whole staff and all the residents were talking about the gorgeous lady except Tom. He had been out of town for a few days and had not been around to see this beautiful Lydia. A knock on my door came one morning as Tom came in with his usual great smile and positive attitude. I filled him in on this new resident and told him that he must meet her. It was my feeling that the meeting would be a match from heaven, and he laughed and laughed.

About a week later, we had a wine-tasting dinner. All of the residents were attending, and the activity center was packed out. Tom was sitting at a table with seven other residents, and across the room sat Lydia with her bridge friends. Lydia saw one of her neighbors sitting next to Tom and wanted to run over and speak to him. When she came to their table, she glanced at Tom and couldn't speak. Tom looked up and became paralyzed for a few seconds. Finally, Lydia's neighbor introduced Tom to Lydia. They both nodded, and Lydia went back to her table. Tom jumped up and almost ran to my table, which was a good distance away from most of the residents. He told me that he had just seen the most beautiful woman in the world and that he was going to marry her! In two weeks, they were married in the chapel with only the preacher, a witness, and me in attendance. They are living happily ever after.

The music man finally came to live at the home. Andy could play at least six instruments, including the banjo! He had played in the symphony in a local town and loved playing his bassoon and other instruments during choir rehearsal. With Sandy playing piano and Andy his instrument, it made the choir sound really professional. The residents were so excited to see Andy every rehearsal because he was always bragging about how well everyone sounded. There were eight men singing bass and tenor and twenty-two ladies singing soprano and alto. The blend was beautiful, and we worked on some very challenging choir tunes.

In the middle of the summer, another alto joined our group. Ellen was from up north and came to live at the home only because her roommate from college was living there. She was seventy-four and had never married. The love for horses and dogs was evident because her apartment was filled with horse blankets and dog pictures. The roommate from college had married an Episcopal priest, and they were a big part of Ellen's life when she moved to the Angel's Nest. As the choir worked on Handel's *Messiah* and other classical music selections, Ellen asked if she could play the flute along with Andy and Sandy. The trio blended very well, and a chamber ensemble was formed. We discovered that, with an ensemble, the choir could miss a few notes and never be noticed because the bassoon or the flute or the piano would drown out any mistakes, making us sound even better.

Ellen's love for music and for learning to play more instruments brought Andy and Ellen together every week for rehearsals. Their friendship grew and grew, and Ellen's knowledge for becoming a great instrumentalist grew as well. After about a year of having some wonderful concerts and a few chamber events, cupid hit Ellen and Andy right smack in the heart. They were rehearsing and having some great conversations over the weeks and months, and one day, Andy told Ellen she needed a husband. Ellen agreed, and about three weeks later, the two were married in the chapel when everyone was at lunch. They wanted a private wedding, so Ellen's roommate suggested that her Episcopal priest husband preside over the ceremony to make it legal. This was a splendid idea, and before anyone knew it, there was another wedding at the Nest!

NANCY'S SENIOR OLYMPIC EVENT

Little Nancy was a very spunky resident at the Angel's Nest Nursing Home. She would come to my office every day and tell me what I needed to do. On one occasion, Ms. Nancy mentioned the Senior Olympic events at one of the junior colleges. She reminded me that it was very important for our nursing home to make an appearance and participate in the upcoming events. Little Nancy had been going to the Senior Olympics for several years and had won gold medals in all of the events that she participated in. Of course, she was the only participant from our facility. We began launching a campaign for all residents to join our Senior Olympic winning team. Little Nancy put signs on the bulletin board. She handed out flyers, and she promised that all residents would receive a gold medal. What I did not realize is that Nancy was choosing the oldest residents in our nursing home to participate. On the first year that I took the bus to Senior Olympics, we had ten residents entering the events. The ages of these residents were eighty to ninety-five years old. The participants ran in age groups of five years—the eighty- to eighty-five-year-olds in one group, the eighty-six- to ninety-year-olds in another group, and the ninety-one- to ninety-five-year-olds in another group. Since Nancy was the captain of the team, she assigned each resident an event to participate in. The amazing and beautiful thing that happened really shocked our nursing home! All ten residents were awarded gold medals because these residents were the only ones participating in their age group. Events from the one-hundred-yard walk to the football throw, the baseball throw, the dart throw, the basketball free throw, and even the horseshoe throw awarded us a gold medal.

All the way home from the Senior Olympic day, we sang the song "Glory Hallelujah"! When we arrived at the front entrance, we were greeted by all of the residents, all of the employees, and our administrator, along with the local newspaper and the mayor of the town! This was a triumphal day for little Nancy, our ten participants, family members, all participants, and the entire town! These famous athletes walked into the dining room and were greeted with a standing ovation and a victorious meal! From that year on, we participated in the Senior Olympics with little Nancy as our fierce leader!

TAPPING AND FLYING

Charlie May was at the Angel's Nest Nursing Home with his wife when she was trying to recover from an illness. She passed shortly after they arrived, and he mourned her death for over a year. He was a pilot and flew his plane every week for fun and would even go to Ole Miss to the ball games and carry a friend with him in his two-passenger single-engine Cessna.

This man loved to dance and play the piano. He only knew one tune on the ivory keys, but since he was eighty years young, it was obvious to us that he once had an entire repertoire of songs that were played for friends and family.

The line dancers were always learning new steps and performing for other facilities in the surrounding areas. The group became famous around town and was asked to perform at the Neshoba County Fair. This made Charlie very happy because he had two cabins at the fair, and the entire dancing group was invited to stay at his cabins for lunch after the dance performance and even listen to some of the politicians while there. The governor came around and invited us to the Governor's Mansion to entertain for an event during the Christmas holidays. All eighteen of us accepted the invitation, and we even had a few more residents join the group when they found out about the invite!

One year, we took the line dancers on a dinner cruise down the Mississippi River on the *Mississippi Queen*. The show for the evening was a group of Japanese dancers in their native dress. After about forty-five minutes of exotic dancing, the group invited the audience to come up and dance with them. Our line dancers leaped to the occasion, and in less than ten minutes, our little Angel's Nest line dancers were teaching this Japanese group how to line dance. The oriental sound of "Boot Scootin' Boogie" was quite a hit, and every person in the banquet hall got up and started line dancing. Charlie had the Japanese director on the stage teaching him how to tap dance! We made history that night by bringing Japanese culture to a country-western flair! The captain of the *Mississippi Queen* brought out the wine and cheese and asked us to stay and teach his crew how to boogie, and Charlie said he would give him tap dance lessons at no charge!

The airplane that Charlie flew was kept in his hangar in Flora. This was not a normal hangar for airplanes. The building had an apartment and a dance floor plus outside seats on a deck along the runway. Music was piped in, out and through the complex. Wherever you ventured out on the property, there was music!

Charlie wanted to take the entire Angel's Nest resident population to the hangar for a cookout, dance, and plane ride. Everyone was thrilled to go, and we had to rent a bigger bus to carry everyone to this fun activity!

Several of the residents had cars, so the caravan headed to Flora one fine day to play! The burgers and chips came with food service. Drinks and snacks hitched a ride with the bus drivers. The line dancers rode in one of the vans that Charlie owned.

When we arrived at the hangar, there were tons of folks already there dancing and touring this most unusual paradise for pilots! Charles had even invited two other men with planes to come join us and take our residents for a plane ride. I think every soul there rode in a plane. One lady had to be helped in, and when she returned, it took four men to assist in getting her back on the ground. She was spellbound and wanted to ride again! A volunteer rang the dinner bell, so she quickly began to head for the meal. This lady really loved to eat, so the second plane ride was put on hold! We had enough food to feed our residents and all fourteen volunteers that came to help with the event. We had so much fun this became an annual affair that spread throughout the area, and the three-hour outing turned into a day in the country with Charles and his line dancers. By 9:00 p.m., the group decided it was time to head back to the home; and each year, the norm was to end the party with line dancing 'til nine! Happy campers they all were every time we headed to that hangar!

LET'S HAVE IT OUTSIDE!

Most of our parties and special events were held inside due to the inclement weather we were always having. During October and November, we tried to have as many outdoor events as possible. Such was the case one year when the activity committee decided we needed a fanfare outdoors in October that we would call the October Fall Festival. A band was hired, and the dining room staff would cater the event. Decorations were plentiful; and as many as twenty of our residents helped decorate and set the festive tables with flowers, pumpkins, gourds, orange tablecloths, and napkins. The dining staff stayed busy bringing all of the food out to the different stations that had been set up hours before the great event. This was a record-breaking attendance for sure, and just about all of the residents signed up to come for the 5:00 p.m. affair!

At 4:45 p.m., a huge dark cloud came over the area, and thunder began to sound all around us. In just two more minutes, the wind and lightning started, and our October Fall Festival was in trouble.

The head chef looked at me and said, "Your call."

I nodded, and we started taking all of the stations inside! Many of the residents began to come to our rescue because they felt sorry for us due to the hard work and preparation that was done by so many for this fun event. In an instant, it seemed we had everything and everyone inside, and we shared the activity room and the dining room with this crowd of wet-but-happy people. A bar was set up in the hallway, connecting the dining room and the activity room. The band began to play next to the bar. Food was being passed out as fast as possible with no waiting lines due to the open bar of margaritas and peach schnapps available for all at no extra charge!

The October Fall Festival turned out to be one of the finest parties ever recorded! Everyone danced, ate, drank, and shared stories with each other. Before we realized it, the hours had flown by, and it was bedtime for most of us! We talked about that event for months! Rain can be a real factor in the lives of the residents at the Angel's Nest Nursing Home. Uh-huh!

THE BANK GOT US IN TROUBLE!

Our local banks, two of them to be exact, were always competing to get the residents' money in their bank. They would host parties, give bingo prizes, and even sponsor day trips and a few overnight trips. Each month, the residents would try to come up with something new that the banks could "give them" that would outdo the other bank.

One bank wanted to host the Croquet Extravaganza that was coming up in a month or so. This was just before Easter, and the bank events planner did not want to spare any expense. She wanted to do something that would hit the local newspaper and spread throughout the county as well as rub the other bank's reputation raw!

Ta-da! The food would be catered by a company in the neighboring town, and martinis would be served in a glass with a beautiful ripe strawberry in the bottom of each drink. This would look elegant, and every table would have linen cloths with spring bouquets to match the linens. The food table would have an enormous centerpiece that would be given away at the end of the event, along with many other elaborate door prizes and a bottle of champagne to the winning team. The bank even hired a master of ceremonies to conduct the entire event. The local newspaper was contacted. Let the games begin. And they did! The music played. The teams hit the ball all over the small field, hitting trees and metal brackets in the ground that housed the outdoor lights, but play continued. Drinks were served to all who attended, and the food was being consumed at a rapid speed. Prizes were handed to those whose names were drawn out of a big glass bowl, and the bank was receiving the compliments and praises from all.

It was time to end this wonderful event. The band left on the city bus. Bank tellers were packing extra supplies and loading them in their vehicles. The master of ceremonies politely made, his exit but none of the residents were leaving their tables. What was wrong? Were they having such a good time that they hated to depart from their friends and neighbors?

One little resident raised her hand and—in her tiny, frail voice—said, "We are all dizzy. I don't think we can walk. Can the maintenance men come and get us and take us to our apartments?"

With great concern, the question was asked if anyone could walk home. Not one person could raise their hand. It took the staff, maintenance, and the bank tellers forty-five minutes to get each resident safely home. One resident said she was drinking those fruit drinks just to get to the beautiful big strawberries at the bottom of the glass.

The bank didn't give any more parties for quite a while, and the residents could not understand why fruit drinks could make you so dizzy!

THE INDOOR
POOL PARTY

The Angel's Nest Nursing Home had an indoor swimming pool that wasn't used very much. Being a creative activity director, I decided it was time for an indoor pool party with food and drinks. The cooking staff fixed sandwiches and chips and little finger foods while the residents decided to bring the drinks. We had ice tea and Bloody Marys. A few of the residents did not know that vodka was in the drink, including me. Having a celery stick and an olive in a drink would lead one to believe that was a healthy concoction.

For the main event of the party, the ladies were dressing as water swans and doing a swan dance in the pool. The men were dressing up as ladies with wigs so that they would not be identified to play a volleyball game in the water with the swans. Looking back, I realize that the men probably brought the Bloody Marys; cannot imagine that a swan would do such a thing.

As the music was playing and the swans were dancing in the water, a new couple came into the swimming area, Nancy and John from New Orleans, Louisiana.

When the men came out of the dressing rooms looking like women and the marine song was playing, Nancy and John looked at each other and said, "Let's call the children and tell them that we are in the right place. This is gonna be great! We will never get bored here."

The pool was heated, and the room was very warm about this time. Bloody Marys were being consumed rapidly by everyone, thinking that they were having a very healthy drink. One of the retired pastors at the village, Bill Basque, started singing and dancing all by himself without any help from anyone. The shocking news is that he could not carry a tune in a bucket. His wife was speechless and turning very, very pale. In a flash, she had the pastor by his ear, dragging him out of the room. We did not see Pastor Basque and his wife for several weeks. We just hoped that they began speaking to one another again. For about a month, they would pass their neighbors in the hall with a brief nod.

Eventually, things got back to normal, we think.

POLICE AND
WOMEN'S DAY

The Angel's Nest Nursing Home organized a mission choir. Each quarter, the choir would travel to other nursing homes or adult day-care facilities to sing to the folks there. We always carried the large bus and the small bus to get all thirty-three of our choir members to a particular place to perform. On one occasion, we accidentally left the piano player and headed off without counting heads. When we reached our destination and found the activity center, it occurred to me that the old piano in the corner of the room was missing our accompanist! I began to panic! No one knew the piano player's phone number since she was a volunteer who lived a good distance from the home. We were about to sing without piano when we heard a voice in the back of the room shout, "I'm here! I'm here! The police chief brought me since my car broke down in front of the police station and I knew I was gonna be late!"

The program was a huge success, and the piano was especially loud that day!

One of our housekeepers came into my office and asked if the choir could come to their Women's Day celebration at the St. Joseph Missionary Baptist Church to entertain the ladies during this special occasion. She explained that this was a fundraiser day for the church. Every lady from each family would come in their best dresses, and when their family name was called, the lady from that family would come to the altar and leave $100 on the offering plate. If a lady did not have $100, the other ladies would help her by donating what they could to make up the difference. There were about fifty ladies in the little church that Saturday, and they were dressed in their finest cotton and linen! Colorful hats matched their dresses, and their shoes were matching as well. We had never seen such beauty in church before. Little did we know that every lady also brought a covered dish, and we were invited to stay for a fabulous meal after the service! When it was our time to perform, I was so spellbound with the congregation I asked the preacher if they would teach us to sing "Swing Low, Sweet Chariot" since it was a black spiritual that had so much feeling. The preacher smiled and nodded to one of his ladies. She rose, went to the piano, and began playing the most beautiful music; and the ladies of the St. Joseph Missionary Baptist

Church began chanting and humming in harmony "Swing Low." I thought the heavenly angels were coming to get us and take us home. The sounds coming out of those ladies were so angelic. Heaven was sounding sweeter and sweeter. We were frozen in awe and admiration as the Holy Spirit moved into that little country church!

When they finished singing, our choir just smiled, and we all said in unison, "Amen!"

Then I said, "Y'alls praying and singing were gifts from God."

We learned so much that day!

THE MATH TEACHER

Bertha Moses, whom we called Lady B, came to the Nest shortly after her husband passed away. This lady had a very robust figure that matched her robust voice. The residents tended to shy away from her because of her aggressive approach to everyone. During most of her conversations, she would point her finger, raise her voice, and shout about how wonderful her husband was. To honor his memory, Lady B wore his clothes every day.

She wore his shirts, his belt, his pants, and his watch. She would wear his shoes. But they were two sizes too large, so they stayed in her room by the front door, all five pairs of them lined up in a row. She made the remark one morning at coffee that, about once every six weeks, she would polish his shoes and talk to him. They had very interesting conversations, and he gave her advice most of the time. When talking with other residents, Lady B would always say, "This is what my husband is advising me to do" or "My husband feels the same way I do about this."

My office was in a direct route to the dining room, so every day around lunchtime, there would be a small group of ladies hiding in my office until Lady B passed by heading to eat lunch. These ladies refused to sit at the same table with Lady B because their conversations would be cut off immediately with tales from the past about Lady B's romance with her late husband and about her excellent teaching skills as a math teacher. They would stay hidden until other residents passed by, assuring them that the dining table would be full and they could sit elsewhere. (As residents came to dine at each meal, the hostess would sit them together when they entered the dining room, so no seats could be saved at any time.)

I suggested to the three ladies to find a fourth whom they could put up with at lunch so they wouldn't have to hide every day in my office, not that I minded it at all. It was very funny, and we laughed a lot while they were in my presence. This seemed to be a good idea, so one of the ladies thought of the best-looking man in the village to call and put me up to call him. He was flattered to be asked to dine with three ladies (who were attractive), and he agreed to do so. This solved the problem, and my office became quiet again.

To go into the dining room, one would have to pass by my office. It never failed that, about once or twice a day, there would be residents in my office hiding from Ms. B. I would try to talk to the residents, and they would hush me and command me to stand at the door and make sure that Ms. B had already passed going to the dining room. They would wait about five more minutes and then head to the dining room for their meal. It was quite obvious that most of the residents were dodging her to avoid conversation after conversation about her husband or her excellent students whom she taught in her math classes. When Ms. B ate with some of the men, it was amazing to see that her demeanor was totally changed to a soft-spoken, very attentive lady. She never remarried. Her epitaph read "Mr. Moses, I am finally coming to join you."

SINGING AND PREACHING AT THE SONSHIP MISSIONARY BAPTIST CHURCH

Gospel music was a lot of fun to sing in our little choir. We even had a gospel quartet who would go to the different churches and old folks' homes and sing favorites like "I'll Fly Away," I'll Meet You in the Morning," "In the Sweet By and By," "Nothing but the Blood," and "Just a Little Talk with Jesus Makes It Right!" Word spread all over the community that we were willing and able to sing anytime and anywhere. The quartet had a bass and tenor with Ms. Edna singing loud soprano and me singing loud alto. Our piano player was a volunteer named Polly who was a staunch Catholic girl that could walk the piano with our hard-shell Baptist hymns! She never turned down any opportunity to play that piano for the choir, the quartet, or any service that required a pianist. Polly was always ready and willing to use her great talent for others!

The choir was asked to entertain at the health fair one year that was held in the shopping mall downtown. We loaded everybody up in vans; and our piano player, Polly, brought a car full of folks with her. We began singing songs like "Blue Suede Shoes" and "Love Me Tender," thus starting to draw a crowd around our thirty-two members of songbirds. The shopping mall was a two-story building, and the second floor was filling up fast with people who were admiring our selected songs. As we began to sing our final song, "I'll Fly Away," the crowd began to clap; and we got faster and faster.

Polly was just about to knock the keys off of the electric piano we had borrowed for this festive event when a big, healthy, robust woman on the second floor leaned over the rail and shouted, "Praise the Lord! Thank you, Jesus! I'm comin'!"

Just at that moment, she started to tumble over the rail, taking two other spectators with her. All three came tumbling down to the first floor and were saved by the hay wagon full of hay below on level one. The theme was Western, and I do believe a miracle happened that day as we saw these folks flying. That song took on a new meaning for us, and we were very particular where we sang it in the future.

Our bus driver heard about the quartet, so he came to me one day and said that the preacher of his church wanted me to lead the women in a Bible devotion on Wednesday night before their revival began that Sunday. He also wanted me to bring the quartet to sing and lead them in some congregational singing. It sounded like an excellent idea because I really did enjoy teaching the Bible to women and our quartet loved to sing. We took several weeks to prepare our songs, and Polly was very excited about going with us! My husband wanted to go to hear the quartet and support me.

When we arrived at the Sonship Missionary Baptist Church, there was not a parking place to be found. We had to park on the street and walk about two hundred yards to get inside. I could not imagine that the church had a parking lot full of women, but it didn't hit me until we entered the sanctuary. There was no room to sit. The pastor greeted us and took us right to the altar where there were six seats behind the pulpit for us, including a seat for my husband. Polly went straight to the piano and began playing some gospel hymns for a prelude. The church members, including men and children, began to clap and sing along with her. This was a pre-revival meeting with all of the church present, and I was to be the preacher! It was too late to back out, but I did not believe in teaching men and women Bible study.

My husband whispered, "Do it, honey. It's too late to back down, and I know you're gonna be in your element."

Well, I was definitely in my element. So the pastor introduced all of us, and the congregation clapped and nodded. Our quartet sang "Swing Low, Sweet Chariot" while the church hummed and chanted. It was glorious. Heaven was opening up, and we were all being blessed. We sang a few more chosen songs, then I proceeded to give a Bible study that was prepared for women. But God led me through it, and with a prayer constantly on my lips and in my heart, the service ended with all of the congregation singing "There's a Sweet, Sweet Spirit in This Place." All of us stayed for the Wednesday night supper, which was one of the best meals ever eaten at any one place. The sweet Christians in that church made us feel loved, and the children had their Bibles in hand and thanked us all for coming. It was a good night!

PHDS FROM LSU

Mary and Bob Weston moved into the Angel's Nest Nursing Home on a sunny day in June. Their reputation had preceded them as being vibrant, active, robust, and very smart! We were all looking forward to meeting them and getting to know them better. They moved into one of the larger apartments, which was actually two small apartments converted into a larger one, which was called a Grande unit. They had the apartment converted into a larger unit because they loved to entertain. Of the two of them, Mary was probably the most active, but Bob had tons of energy as well. Bob was always the gopher between the two. You would see him running down the halls going to this and going to that for his wife, Mary.

The first thing Mary wanted when she came to the home was to organize a welcome committee with her being the chairperson. She began to organize this group and added four couples and six singles to be a part of what would be known as the best welcome committee in the South. As new residents moved into the home, Mary would assign either a couple to greet the new couple or a single resident to greet the single resident moving in. The newcomers would be taken to lunch and then given a tour of the village and also would be invited to any activities for the week. In the welcome committee were some who cooked or baked special goods to give to the newcomers on their first day, and in some cases, a full breakfast would be prepared, especially if the couple or new single had come in late at night.

Everyone wanted to be on Mary Weston's welcome committee because things were always bustling with good deeds and compliments to follow!

The Westons were definitely pacesetters because every activity that they attended was enhanced by their beautiful costumes! They had lived in Mexico for about five years. So of course, when we had the Cinco de Mayo party in May, the Westons furnished all the decorations and even sombreros for the men and maracas for the ladies! Mary was a wonderful cook, so she prepared several Mexican dishes for the event. And the couple did several Mexican dances to entertain us! Every time they walked into a room, the residents would applaud because of their energy and ability to please the crowd! Mary even taught Spanish to any of the residents who wanted to learn the language.

Every time we had a play, Bob and Mary would try out and, in most cases, play the leading roles because they were naturals at just about everything they attempted to do! They even donated a sewing machine that was used to make costumes for many of the plays with Mary leading the charge!

I really believe that happy hour was created when Bob and Mary moved to the home. Every Friday around 4:00 p.m., they would invite any resident who wanted to attend a chance to see their home and enjoy drinks and hors d'oeuvres. They did this all the years that they were at the home, and after their deaths, this continued as an activity in the activity center. The residents were never asked to BYOB or to bring any refreshments during the four o'clock hour in their home, but everyone was treated like royalty and would leave smiling and wanting to come again.

Bob and Mary were very wealthy, and they had money in all of the major banks in the town. It did not take them long to get each bank involved in the community of the nursing home. Each week, the banks would come out on a given day on a given time for about an hour to service our residents and to help them with any of their banking needs. Of course, each bank became very competitive, and Mary suggested that they have bank parties for the residents to get more business. The parties began small but grew to be very fancy and elaborate! About every other month, the banks would have another party, and they would bring gifts to be drawn by the residents! This, of course, helped the activity program tremendously; and the home developed a reputation of being the place where party animals lived! It was exciting to know that we were not in an old nursing home but a place where you could come and get active and stay active for a long, long time!

In 1997, when I decided to marry, the Westons, of course, helped bring all of the residents to our home for the tea party after the wedding. They had planted white streamers and balloons all the way from the village to our home, which was seven miles away. There was no chance of anyone getting lost and not attending the celebration because the Westons made sure it was a great success!

Speaker of the Month was an activity where outside speakers were invited to come to the home and speak on different subject matters. There were politicians, governors, lawyers, architects, librarians, firemen, policemen, pastors, teachers, doctors, nurses, and even coaches that would come and spend time with us as our speaker for the month. Bob and Mary would always take the speaker or speakers each month to lunch in our dining room, and then they were invited to their apartment for coffee and dessert. It was always hospitality at its finest with the Westons.

FATHER MAHONEY'S BLESSING

Father Mahoney was one of the priests who lived at the Nest. He was everyone's friend. When the residents went on a field trip to one of the casinos for a free lunch, our priest was the first one to sign up to go. I cannot recall a trip to Vicksburg, Philadelphia, or Natchez that he did not attend. He suggested an overnight trip to Tunica, which was about four hours away. We would have to have twenty-five in order to go. To be sure that the trip was on, Father Mahoney paid the way for several residents in order for us to have the twenty-five needed to go. This was an overnight trip where the casino gave us free meals and a great discount on our rooms. We were also given $25 each to play the slots. When it was time for us to leave, I counted everyone on the bus, and guess who was not with us? You guessed it—our very own Father Mahoney. The assistant activity director went with me to find our dear friend, knowing he was having fun somewhere! And sure enough, there he was on the one-dollar slot machine giving it every dollar he had! We had to practically tear him away from the slot machine because he was winning, or so he said, a lot of money. Ha-ha! When we returned to the bus, Father Mahoney started handing out dollar bills to everyone on the bus. And of course, we all gave him a sitting ovation with loud applause! We gave him the nickname of Mr. Lucky and made sure he went with us every time we planned a trip to the casino!

Before our September wedding, I asked Father Mahoney if he would come and bless our wedding since this was a common thing for priests to do. He gladly agreed. My Baptist preacher at the time was not too pleased about this since he never had a Catholic priest standing beside him at a wedding. He finally agreed to come and let Father Mahoney bless the wedding at the end of the ceremony. Only family members attended the actual wedding, which was held in our backyard, but all the residents were invited to attend a tea party afterward. All of our five dogs and eight horses were standing close by during the ceremony. So when it was time to bless the wedding, Father Mahoney blessed me, my husband, and all of our animals!

I told Father Mahoney that we were going to have the tea party, and he asked if there would be tea with a kick. He came early to check out the tea with a kick.

I let him sample the tea, and he said, "Where is the kick?"

I pointed to the kitchen cabinet, and he went over and took the vodka from the cabinet and filled the punch with more kick. The bus came over with all of our residents right after the wedding, and we had a great tea party. The weather was perfect, and all of our animals sat or stood at the gate while the residents complimented them for being so well mannered.

When our dearly beloved Father Mahoney passed away, he left $1,000 to his nephew with instructions: "This money is to be spent at the casinos. Give it away if you have to, but enjoy it!" The nephew, whom we will call Patrick, also lived at the Nest.

He came by my office one day and dropped a $100 bill on my desk. "You've got to help me spend this money. We've got to go to the casino and get rid of it!"

I quickly told him to get that money off of my desk before I got fired! He smiled, grabbed the hundred-dollar bill, and said he would save it for a rainy day. I was grateful and pleased to have Patrick as a dear friend and conversationalist. Being Catholic, Patrick would come into my office at least once a week with a question to ask me since I was at the time a converted Presbyterian from a foot-washing, hard-shell Baptist background. We agreed to disagree and listen to each other's response to many wonderful questions about the Bible and Bible teachers and prophets from the Old and New Testaments. To my surprise, Patrick knew many of the Bible stories; and he gave detailed outlines of Matthew, Mark, Luke, and John. One of his favorites was Peter, so we discussed him more than the others. I miss my friend and those wonderful discussions!

STATE CHAMPIONSHIP
IN THE BAG!

Our sons played football, and the youngest was in the state finals for the first time his senior year. This game was the highlight of the year, so it was the responsibility of family and friends to get the crowds there to cheer the team to victory. I knew that the sisters and many of the residents at the nursing home would love to attend this exciting game! The pep squad of the century would arrive from the Angel's Nest Nursing Home, and our team would win because all of the sisters came with their sweaters and coats and team spirit to cheer them on.

This plan was quickly put into action because the players ran onto the field with about two hundred fans yelling and greeting them with high fives and words of encouragement. The sisters wore their habits so the players would know that many prayers were being sent up every play of the game!

It wasn't snowing, but the wind would take you away if you weren't tied to the bleachers. Everyone wrapped up with blankets, coats, winter boots, and hot chocolate. The cold weather did not affect the sisters because their mother's house was up north and they were used to the cold temperatures and gusts of bitter wind. One sister wore a sweater and did not even button it. She assured me that her body was warm, and each time she yelled for our team, she would almost break out with perspiration.

At halftime, as the players ran off the field, all of the twelve sisters ran down to the fence near the gate where the players would pass through to the field house; and they screamed for the team and gave them all high fives! At the time, the score was 12 us, 14 them.

The second half of the game proved to be almost too exciting for us to bear!

Our team received the ball; and our running back made a forty-six-yard run, broke through a two-man tackle, and made it to their twenty-yard line! Two plays later, we scored and ran in for a two-point conversion, changing the score to 20 us, 14 them. The crowd roared, and the game ended after our team blocked an attempted field goal from the opposing team! We were the new state champs, and we had the trophy to prove it!

My son came running to us, and he hugged all of the residents and thanked the sisters for getting the Big Man's help! It was a night to remember!

NURSES TO NUNS

The sisters of the Catholic faith owned the Angel's Nest Nursing Home, along with many other facilities, schools, and hospitals. They were always having fundraisers and including the staff to help.

One day, the head nun asked some of us to participate in a fundraiser that involved one of their large hospitals. We were to dress up like nuns and go around to the nursing homes and hospitals singing to help get donations.

We were called the Singing Nuns, and this idea caught on like gangbusters. So many businesses would call on us to come and sing to their employees, thus aiding them when money was needed for a good cause. It seemed like, every week or so, we would be called on to put our act together and sing. The administrator loved the idea because it helped market our little nursing home to the public!

The habits (nun's clothing) were heavily cleaned and starched, and each week we would have to take our bor-rowed habits to be cleaned. This became rather expensive, so our administrator told us to give these habits to the house-cleaning department and not take them to the cleaners, cutting our expenses down a great deal. There was no problem with this method until, one week, house cleaning gave us our habits and they were all pink instead of pure white. I had accidentally left a box of red menthol cough drops in the pocket of my habit, which turned us into pink nuns. Pushed for time and thinking the pink looked pretty awesome, we went ahead and put the pink habits on, ran out to sing at one of the local businesses, and returned to work. Word spread fast about the new nuns in town from the pink order. The head nun gave us a visit to find out who had stolen our "show." When we explained the situation to her, she fell out laughing. Our jobs were not put on the line!

I do recall on one occasion we were running late to an event that was held at the hospital. As we came into the parking area, there were no parking places, but a guard was standing nearby. We quickly drove up to him (already dressed in our borrowed habits) and asked him to please find us a parking place because we were very late for an important meeting. He spoke to us with much reverence, bowed his head, and led us to a parking place next to the front door.

We thanked him and said, "God bless."

Many months later, I was having lunch with the head nun at the hospital and gave her my confession about the parking space. She laughed and said that I could borrow her habit any time I felt the need or when I was really in a hurry. She made me feel a whole lot better after telling me the story of her being able to get out of having speeding tickets because she was wearing her habit.

"The Lord has been watching over me," she said, "and I am truly grateful."

MRS. KELLY

One of our beloved residents at the nursing home was a very interesting lady named Mrs. Kelly. She loved her cigarettes. At the time, it was no problem smoking at the nursing home as long as you did not offend others with your smoke. The nursing home went on a field trip one day to the casino in Vicksburg. Mrs. Kelly was outside smoking when the bus was being loaded. All heads were counted, and the bus took off. After about twenty minutes of driving back to the nursing home, the bus driver received a phone call. It was Mrs. Kelly. She was panicky because we had left her behind.

In her soft, sweet voice she said, "Somebody please come and pick me up. The bus left me here, and please bring me some cigarettes when you come."

Another time, the residents went to the small pond fishing and to the little cabin next to the pond for a picnic. Mrs. Kelly came over wearing one of her lovely dresses. The residents were sitting at the picnic tables, eating their food, and a small voice was heard in the distance.

"Help! I need help!"

It was Mrs. Kelly! She had slipped into the lake, dress and all as she tried to pull in a large fish that was on her fishing line. Before we could get to her, Mr. Werley was trying to pull Mrs. Kelly out of the pond. He didn't have much luck because he only weighed about ninety-eighty pounds soaking wet. Just before he went in, headfirst, we managed to pull him out along with Mrs. Kelly, and all she wanted was her fish and her wet cigarettes! It took Mr. Werley about a week to completely dry out! The kitchen took the seven-pound fish in and cooked it for the supper meal, along with a few more fish caught that day. By the time the story was told in town, the fish weighed fifteen pounds, and it took five people to pull it in!

ALMA'S TEMPER TANTRUM

The Potters lived at the Angel's Nest Nursing Home and were quite active around the place. Alma was into arts and crafts, always making doll dresses for her porcelain doll collection. She came down to my office all the time showing me the latest dress she had made for her newest doll. If my count is correct, she had about twenty different porcelain dolls ranging from the Bebe dolls to five varieties of the Madam Alexander doll to Big Fat Happy Baby and, of course, the rare antique googly-eyed dolls! She was very proud of her skill of dressmaking, but it became boring after a spell. Her next adventure was going to be making these dolls from porcelain and painting them herself. There was a problem: no kiln at the Angel's Nest Nursing Home. She asked me many times to buy a kiln, and I always replied that we did not have the budget for one or a place to put it.

William, Alma's husband, was a retired professor from one of the state universities; and his hobby was riding on trains. He was always gone on a train ride, so Mrs. Alma had a whole lot of time on her hands—a whole lot of time! She would come down to the craft room and bug Mr. Johnny every day. Mr. Johnny was a resident who volunteered to run the craft room and make glass clocks and jewelry in his spare time. She even asked him to buy a kiln, and he always said no!

One fair day, I was having a pleasant conversation with a veteran resident in my office, and here came Mrs. Alma bursting in like a wild buffalo being chased by Indians. She threw her body, all 240 pounds of it, on my desk, hands planted firmly and her head in a paralyzed lock glued to my eyes. My veteran friend jumped up to escape, and I grabbed his arm and planted him back in the chair to my left that was almost touching the raging bull, Mrs. Alma. He sat motionless while Mrs. Alma yelled at me with everything she could muster up for a loud, intimidating voice.

The one-way conversation went like this: "I want a kiln, and I want it now! I know we have the money to buy one because we have wine every Friday night in the dining room, and being a foot-washing, hard-shell Baptist teetotaler, I want my share of that vulgar money to buy me a kiln! Now you get with it and buy me one!"

In my very quiet tone, I replied: "Mrs. Alma, if you will take your request right now to our administrator and tell her exactly what you just told me, in the same energy level you are in now, I just know you will get that kiln!"

In two weeks, the new kiln arrived!

THE SUGAR MOMMA

Don Loper came to the Angel's Nest at a time when there was thirty-ladies-to-one-man ratio. Therefore, he was a very popular resident. All the ladies were out to get Don Loper, not because he had a lot of money, but because he could drive at night and because he was very charming and witty. He made everyone laugh with his funny stories and his original jokes. He would come into my office almost every day with a brand-new idea. Some of his ideas were too wild to pursue, but most of them we pursued. For example, he wanted some of the men to dress up like the California raisins and dance at one of our parties. This sounded like a great idea. All of the men there, eight at the time, wanted to be one of the California raisins. The costumes were really easy. We used black garbage bags, white tennis shoes, white gloves, and oversized sunglasses. When the music came on, "Heard It Through the Grapevine," everyone roared with laughter because the men were the hit of the night. This started a sequence of events for the famous Don Loper. Everyone waited each week to see what he had planned for us and who would be involved.

Drama was his strong point. He really wanted to do a play, so we decided to write one together. This play involved about twenty of the residents, and it was in a doctor's office. The name of the play was *What You Got?* It was so funny that we decided to write more plays and call our drama group the Punch Line Theater. About every year, we would put on a new play, and we involved three or four of our residents to help us write and edit them.

These plays will be included at the end of this book for your pleasure. During one of the plays, Don Loper met a very happy and glamorous lady who could not keep her eyes or hands off of him. When Don found out that this lady had more money than the Clintons, he latched on to her.

Dorothy Davis was a very happy lady strutting down the hall every day bragging on her precious Donnie. Most of the time, she just called him precious. They went everywhere together. They took trips to Europe and all over the United States and ate at very expensive restaurants all the time. We hardly ever saw Don Loper. If we did, he was with his significant other, Dorothy Davis. Donnie loved baseball, and so did Dorothy. So they went to all the baseball games. Because Don could drive at night, Dorothy would buy a new car every year for their travels.

One day, Don came into my office with his tongue and lips down on his chest. I asked him what was wrong.

He replied, "That Dorothy is just crazy! She makes me so mad. She gave me that brand-new Cadillac!"

And I said, "That is a good thing, right? What is wrong with that?"

And he said, "She's gonna make me pay for the tag. I ain't gonna do it! No, sir, I ain't gonna pay for that tag!"

I said, "How much is the tag?"

And he said, "$386. I'm gonna give her that car back, and I ain't gonna pay it! She's crazy if she thinks I will. She's got money coming out of her ears, so I am not gonna pay for that tag! I think that woman is plain crazy!"

I told Don, if he thought she was crazy, he ought to break up with her! Oh, my goodness! That was the wrong thing to say!

His quick reply went something like this: "Lord, have mercy! I'm not about to break up with that woman. If I did, she'd cut me off! No, no, I ain't gonna be doing something that stupid!"

MR. CROFT'S CRAFTY
SITUATION

Jay and Minnie Croft moved into the Nest when they were only sixty-two years young! Jay had a farm, but it was fifty miles away. He needed something to do with his spare time while his wife, Minnie, played cards with the ladies and joined several committees to keep her very busy. The craft room needed some special attention, and Jay was just the person to get in there and organize the system and create new ideas. He was a worker bee and loved to stay busy. If he wasn't in the craft room, he was on the Airdyne bike in the workout room or walking around the lake. He began to learn all about glass cutting, stained glass, melting glass, and decals on glass; and he took ceramics to a new level by purchasing new molds and making some of his own. He even designed clocks and color schemes for necklaces and earrings for the ladies and sports cups for the Ole Miss, Mississippi State, and Southern Mississippi fans. He was considered the handyman to everyone because he would put new batteries in everything—watches, flashlights, clocks, hearing aids, and remote controls—and he glued picture frames, lamps, antiques, or whatever needed fixing. Jay was the man to get it done!

After about six months, I gave Jay the title of director of the craft room. He was in charge! Everything that was done could be run by Jay, and he would make the decisions.

Now, if there was a certain new resident who moved in and donated paints, pictures, art supplies, sculpture tools, etc., Jay would run to my office with a giant smile on his face and say, "Come quick! You won't believe what we just got for our craft room!"

It didn't take long for our little craft room to fill up fast. Residents would come in and learn how to pour slip (mud for the ceramics) and actually create beautiful items with Jay's help. He was so much fun to be around that several of our artists brought their material down, and Jay found them a table to work on. There have been as many as eight residents in that little craft room at one time, with Jay in his corner playing classical music, smiling and encouraging passersby to come on in and look at all the original art and craft ideas. We decided to have an art and craft show at least once a year, and sometimes twice a year to sell the wonderful items made in that little craft room by Jay and his followers.

Everything started to have order and a permanent place to rest, like the molds for ceramics, the canvases and paint for the art classes, and the many, many bottles of acrylic, oil, and watercolor paint that used to sit on a table with no rhyme or reason. Jay categorized everything and made a notebook so that anyone looking for a certain mold or a certain bottle of paint could go straight to the notebook and find it without any confusion. He truly was a lifesaver for us all. From 8:00 a.m. until noon, he was working in the craft room. After lunch and a nap, he would return for an hour or two, and then Minnie would come by and get him. Off they would go to their apartment for supper. After supper, you would see them walking down the hall and into the activity room for a night of Mexican Train with other residents. Jay would speak to everyone, then march back to the craft room to finish some project he was working on. When residents would come by after their 5:00 p.m. supper in the dining room, they would stick their heads in the craft room door, and Jay would greet many of them with a joke or two or show them his new project and tell them just how he created it. The little bits of colored glass melted down to form beautiful and original drops of overlapping colors were used to create necklaces, earrings, and bracelets.

We all believe, one day, his original glass creations will make him famous around the world. He took much pride in his creations and handling the craft room.

One day, while Jay and Minnie were on a trip with their children, Mrs. Alma, who is mentioned in this book, decided that she could run things as efficiently or even better than Jay. So she reorganized all of the paints, and she brought her porcelain doll molds down to be stored in the craft room on the shelves with the ceramic molds. She did not wait to discuss this with Jay, and being the anxious person that she was, Mrs. Alma spent several days repositioning *everything*! This occurred on a Saturday and Sunday while I was at home or at church. The powers that be did give me weekends off most of the time. Jay came back on Monday. When I walked into my office at 8:15 a.m., he was sitting by my office door and was a deep shade of blood red! I asked him if he was all right.

He said, "Hell no, I'm not all right. I'm fixing to kill a resident, and I wanted to tell you before I did it."

I began to question him, and the story began. We went to the craft room, and it looked as if a group of dolls had moved in. There was lace everywhere and about thirty spools of yarn on one shelf with at least one hundred yards of material on other shelves. Porcelain-doll molds were written on his inventory sheets and not typed in. Jay typed everything himself on his computer and made every change and correction with the Roman font, 16. He almost threw the notebook out the door, and he was so red and shook so much he couldn't speak. I suggested that, before he killed the poor woman, we should try to undo the damage and find a corner for her items. I could have maintenance add a few shelves in one area opposite his area that might work out. He agreed but told me to talk to her so there wouldn't be a killin' or a hangin'! We sorta laughed, and I called to put a work order in for the shelves immediately. Mrs. Alma had a doctor's appointment, thank the Lord, and we were able to put everything in an orderly fashion before she walked in.

When she did enter the craft room just before lunch, her mouth flew wide open; and as she was about to speak, Jay said to her in a very loud and firm voice, "Mrs. Alma, if you don't like it, you can go to hell!"

A calmness came over us all, and she just nodded and held one of her baby dolls as she left.

NOW...ABOUT MY MOMMA

My momma came to the Nest in 2005. It took some trickonometry to get her here, but it worked. Daddy had passed, and Momma was holding down the farm, thinking she would have some of the grands living there and taking care of her. But that plan did not work out. Several of the ladies at the Nest played Rook, Momma's favorite card game— Momma's only card game. She would play Rook with her sisters and brothers all night and into the morning every time they came to the farm for a visit. I called Momma and asked her if she wanted to come and play Rook with some ladies here. She jumped in the car and came, bringing her brown bag lunch, thinking the game would last more than a few hours.

Grace, one of the ladies playing Rook with Momma, said, "Why aren't you living here?"

So Momma turned and yelled across the room, "Daughter, can I afford to live here?"

I smiled and said, "Sure, Momma, as soon as we sell the house and about fifteen acres of the farm."

In three weeks, Momma was moving into the Angel's Nest Nursing Home!

Being a country bumpkin, Momma adjusted quite well. She was a very proud Southern lady who expressed herself pretty often and told everyone how the Lord had gotten her to the Nest. She always told me I was working in a Nest of Angels! She sure had that right! The Catholic nuns were very special, and they all loved Momma! She would bake them one of her pecan pies about once a month to take to the convent; and every time she saw the head nun, it was praises for hiring her daughter and building a wonderful place for folks to live, especially those poor old ladies like herself who had lost their husbands.

The first week, Momma was trying to adjust to community living, but she had to iron out a few wrinkles. She would drop in to see me a little too often, so we had to have an orientation about my job and her habits. She came in one day with a grocery list and handed it to me. I smiled and said that the bus was going to the store the next day at 8:30 a.m. and 1:30 p.m., so she could sign up at the front desk and go shopping with the other residents. She grabbed the list and shook her head as she scampered out the door at a rapid pace. Another time, she called me and wondered if I needed to come to her apartment and take a nap. She thought I was working way too hard. I explained in a calm voice that, if I came to her apartment before it was time to clock out, I would be fired on the spot. She never asked me to come visit before my workday was over again.

Momma had a touch of vanity—or maybe she was just a very proud lady—because she told her sister, who lived in Arab, Alabama, that every morning, after she had her oatmeal and one cup of hot water (coffee was not good for her) and one-half banana, she would put her makeup on and a cute outfit that I had helped her purchase at the local dress shop and she would leave her apartment for the day.

Her sister said, "You mean you wear makeup every day?"

Momma replied, "Doris, we only have a few good-looking men here, and I'm gonna get one of 'em. All the old women here wear makeup, so I'm falling right in with 'em!"

In February, we always had a valentine's dance. With the ratio being thirty to one, the men were very popular at the dances. I even brought some local men from the churches in to dance with the ladies. The Knights of Columbus always helped us out when we had dances so the ladies would feel very special and not get left out during our dances, which we had at least three times a year: Valentine's

Day, New Year's Eve, and in September when we had a "Night in Paris" of dancing and dining.

I was going down the hall inviting all the men to the valentine's dance when one of our very handsome residents said to me, "I'll go if you get your momma to go with me."

Now let me say clearly that this man, Don Hammond, was a very popular man that all the ladies swooned over. He was very handsome, and the only little fallback he had was his voice. Cancer had taken his vocal cords, but he wore a man's infinity scarf, which looked like a tie but more comfortable. His voice was a bit slurred, but it never affected the attention he received from all of the ladies. Don always had a partner for the evening meal. Many times, it was the same lady for about a week, then another lady would enter the picture. Now, about Momma: She always played hard-to-get; and when a man approached her, she would smile, say a few words, then sashay down the hall with her little prissy walk that I'm sure she practiced many times, and go about her business in the exercise room or library. She always looked busy even though her mind might be somewhere else.

After work one day, I stopped by to see Momma and ask her if she wanted to have her first date. When I told her it was with Don Hammond, she let out a yell and said she would go if he asked her himself. Well, he did, and they were the talk of the night with their matching outfits on. She found out what he was wearing; and the next day, we went shopping for a red blouse, black pair of pants, black vest, and red shoes. I have to admit, they were really a cute couple. Don and Del were the hottest couple around for many months. They began to eat lunch and dinner together. Every night, Don would walk Momma home, and they would take the stairs so she could get a good night's kiss behind the door. Momma never let Don come to her apartment because she did not want the neighbors to gossip! I think she went to Don's apartment a few times on a Sunday afternoon to watch a football game or two with the front door always open. She loved Joe Montana and really loved the game of football probably because my sons played football beginning in the fourth grade through college, and she would go to every game possible. Football was as important to her as a good Rook game. My boys would come over and play Rook with Momma on Friday nights after football season while she still lived on the farm. It was her favorite time with them. If they spent the night, she would have pancakes with Blackburn molasses and a pound of bacon cooked for them when they woke up.

Don talked Momma into going to his church with him on Sunday mornings. This lasted for about three months, then she told him it would be better and safer for them to not drive off campus. She explained to him that his driving was dangerous and several times they almost hit other cars. He then confessed that his eyesight was not what it used to be, so he thanked her. They worshipped on Sunday at the Nest with the visiting preacher from a local Baptist church.

Momma's sister, Doris, was always calling her and wanting her to get a car and drive to Arab, Alabama, to stay a month with her for a really good visit. Momma had given my youngest son her car when she moved into the Nest.

In the past when Momma would go see Doris, she would work like a Trojan cleaning and cooking for Doris, then they would play Rook into the early morning hours with their oldest brother, Dewey. Well, Momma came to my office one morning with that grin, which told me she was up to no good, and told me she wanted to go buy a car on my lunch break. I told her to give me a little time and she would get a call from me shortly. With panic mode, I began to pray and ask God to help me deal with my eighty-two-year-old momma! He answered my prayer immediately. In a few hours, I gave Momma a call, and she came rushing into my office. As calmly as possible, from my copy machine, I handed Momma fourteen pages and explained to her that it was impossible for me to take off from my job to go and help with the purchase of a vehicle. But if she would read carefully the following pages on the expenses and details of owning a car, then I would take her on my day off, and we would attempt to get the vehicle of her choice.

I didn't see my momma for three days.

On a Friday, she stormed into my office with the fourteen pages of information, threw the papers on my desk, and said, "You knew just how to get me, didn't you? Forget about the damn car. I'd rather buy clothes and stay here. After all, Doris owes me about a dozen visits anyway!"

Momma never mentioned a car again!

OUR LITTLE MS. SUNSHINE

The Nest was growing so fast that it was obvious we needed some volunteers to help us with bingo, parties, day trips, and other activities. Someone gave me the name of a fire-cracker lady, whom we will call Sparky. She was a realtor in the area that everyone knew. I wanted to contact her and try to convince her to become our volunteer coordinator. When we met, it was very obvious that she was definitely a firecracker with enough energy to set off a rocket. Her personality was exuberant, and her smile was contagious. She definitely knew everyone at the Nest, and her source of contacts was unlimited. Sparky came to the Nest for two weeks and laid out a program for us to implement that would satisfy the criteria without even having the lead of a director. This lady was incredible but way too busy to stop her daily routines and join our little group. She promised me that, in the future, she would see me again. I hugged her and waved goodbye, thinking I would never see her again.

About two years had passed when this ray of sunshine came strolling down the hall with her redheaded husband, Jeb. Sparky had coal-black hair and dark eyes as big as silver dollars. Her skin was olive. I think she was either Lebanese or from Spain. She was striking with her dark features; and her sweet husband, Jeb, was fair skinned with freckles and bright-red hair. He had a very bubbly personality and a smile that warmed the whole room.

They had just moved into the Nest and wanted to meet and greet everyone! Sparky joined the choir and brought about twelve members with her by going to their apartment, and using her persuasive manner, she reeled them in. She even helped welcome everyone to the village when they moved in and worked some with the volunteers to make their time more effective.

This lady could cook anything. She carried food to sick folks, neighbors, new residents, and those moving to another area. Sparky knew the lady who owned the most expensive dress shop in town, so she talked the owner into having a style show at the Nest. This was a huge success, and it became a yearly activity with the models being residents. Sparky helped choose the clothes and accessories as well as being the master of ceremonies for each style show.

We would have wine and cheese following the show, and if anyone purchased outfits that the models were wearing, the shop gave a 20 percent discount on any purchase. News of these style shows spread all around the city, and before long, we had other shops bargaining for the slot. One shop had men's clothing, so of course, several couples modeled when we reached out to other vendors and made the shows more interesting by bringing the men aboard.

Water aerobics was very popular at the Nest. We were paying a lady to come and teach the class. Each resident paid $20 a month to attend this class three times weekly.

After Sparky had been in the class a month, she came to me and said, "Let me teach this class for free. These residents don't need to pay for this. I know this routine backward, and I'll give 'em a really good workout free of charge."

The next month, Sparky was our new water aerobics instructor, and the class doubled in size. Even a few of the men started attending, and you couldn't beat the price!

Now Sparky and I had a really close relationship. She would come into the office at least once or twice a week, and we would network with ideas and come up with new activities. Travel Club was created, and we took the residents on overnight trips every spring and fall. Being the bubbly and energetic resident that Sparky was, she helped me write and edit plays that were performed by our residents at the Nest. Sparky always played the main character in every play mainly because she could remember her lines when others struggled with theirs. She also had a strong voice and could change her characters in a split second. Folks loved to come to see the Punch Line Theater plays that still go on at present. I do believe that our Sparky is still in those plays. She will never grow old and might outlive us all.

At eighty-something, she still looks like a teenager and even acts like one! One thing I can always count on, Sparky knows the words to every song ever written; so when I'm leading our choir in a program, our Sparky is always singing her heart out, smiling at the entire audience, and sharing her love for singing with everyone. She is contagious!

DELTA DAWN

One of our firecracker residents was Delta Dawn. She was four feet, eight inches, in height and had enough energy for twelve folks! This little lady played bridge. She was going to be sure that every person she knew played bridge as well! Delta volunteered to give bridge lessons for beginner, intermediate, and advanced players. This was an activity that spread like wildfire, and in just a few short months, there were enough bridge players for duplicate and party bridge tournaments. Delta always provided the prizes, and my job was to provide the little sheets of paper to tally scores. I was never a bridge player, so the language was and still is foreign to me. Our Ms. Delta became known throughout the city, and in just a year, she had our little nest in some bridge tournaments at the local country club. The next year, twelve of our group took a cruise for a week playing in bridge tournaments. In time, we were known as the place to live and play bridge.

Delta was a great cook, and when she was not at the bridge table, she was in her kitchen cooking a new dish for her third cookbook. Her recipes were tried and proven to be delicious by our kitchen staff and head chef. Delta would take recipes to our chef, and the next week, we were all sampling her dishes and giving a critique on these three-by-five cards at each table. If the food was rated excellent or very good, Delta would use the recipe in her new cookbook. If the dish was rated good or average, she would eliminate it and try something else or add more seasoning to make it flavor friendly for us. She thought the best way to critique would be through our residents simply because of the many complaints that would come to the food committee from so many unhappy or picky folks. Delta was the chairman of the food committee, so this gave her first-hand knowledge about the food and ideas for creating new dishes and fabulous desserts. Her chocolate-vanilla crème cheese pie with walnuts and a scoop of vanilla ice cream topped the list.

Everyone craved her pies but demanded the chocolate-vanilla crème cheese pie the most! Delta sold her cookbooks across the nation, but she always had a book signing at the Nest to allow the residents' first choice. Plus she would give a cooking demonstration of one new recipe at every book signing. We loved our Delta Dawn and miss her delicious food and that wonderful smile she gave every time a bridge game was played!

MADAM PRESIDENT

Lucy Love came to us after serving many years as the president of the American Red Cross. This lady knew protocol like no other. She taught me about organizational teams, committees, peer groups, ad hoc committees, volunteer services, proper grammar, spell-check, finding more in the *Webster Dictionary* instead of asking too many questions, and on and on. I soaked her up like a sponge every time she came to see me or when I called and asked if I could come to see her. We became fast friends and respected each other immensely. She always told me that no question is a dumb question. Just ask it and remember the answer. I remember her telling me that fear was a product of the unknown; so it was imperative that we learn as much as possible about people, places, and things. Lucy would get so frustrated at the way things were handled at our Nest. She always said that so much more could get done if committees were formed and active in their duties. This lady was so convincing that, in just a short time, we had thirty-two activity committees with three to seven people on each committee with a chairman and a cochairman. Each committee had an objective and mission statement. They would meet once a month and leave the meetings with goals and evaluations from the last month. The activity groups began to really make a difference in day-to-day activities; thus, the attendance for the different activities doubled and tripled in some cases.

Bingo grew from 35 to 120 in just two months because we had twelve couples calling bingo but rotating on and off so that no one had to call two weeks in a row. The travel club grew from 12 to 24 in six months, and we began to take more overnight trips with many more day trips. The meet-and-greet group became the happy hour club and met every Friday from 4:00 p.m. to 5:00 p.m.

This group had to move into the big activity center because the attendance outgrew the piazza cafe and at least seven tables of eight per table started coming on a regular basis. The coffee klatch morning group tripled because Lucy made the suggestion of getting our bakers to commit to baking cookies or muffins once a week for the coffee drinkers. She even talked the major bank into bringing donuts every Wednesday to our coffee klatch. Wow!

On Wednesdays, we would have over forty residents for coffee and donuts!

Lucy Love became our first woman president of the residents' association at the Nest. Without pulling all of her hair out, she finally convinced the council members (six of them including the vice president and secretary) to back her up when she appointed chairmen for the following new committees: the Good Things Better Committee, the Green Thumb Committee, the Library Committee, the Food/Fellowship Committee, and the Welcome Committee. Each committee would have five members and meet once a month. During her two-year term as president, she helped the Nest grow by leaps and bounds. A new area was created for the library because more books were donated, and a simple card system was put in place, adding a computer program to simplify the inventory of books. The Good Things Better Committee brought wonderful ideas to enhance the living areas, including a croquet court and a seven-hole putting green along with gorgeous Christmas decorations throughout the Nest inside and lights on the outside. The Green Thumb Committee began growing wonderful flowers at every entrance and placed large potted plants throughout. The place was becoming a paradise from the inside all the way to the entrance on the outside. The Nest was featured in one of the local magazines for being one of the most attractive retirement centers in the South.

Lucy Love will always be remembered for the brilliant ideas that she put into action, and I will always remember her for showing me how to make a mean martini with one olive and one miniature clear onion. My sincere thanks go to Lucy for teaching me how to grow and open up my mind to new ideas and rigid protocol when needed to get out of my comfort zone and explore the impossible and accept the reasonable.

MASTER OF MANY

Dr. David Manhueser gave the Nest a big boost in academics when he began to share his skills and knowledge with us. We all thought he was a shy man who wanted to keep to himself. This was far from the truth. Dr. M just needed time to organize his private library and adjust to his new lifestyle. Three months after his arrival, he came into my office and wanted to share some of his ideas and thoughts with me. After an hour of brainstorming, we had created several new activities for our residents.

Poet's Corner

The group met once a month, and poems would be read and/or created by each resident participating. Dr. M lead this group and shared his own book of poems with everyone. He started out with about three for his first meeting, and as the poems flowed from each resident, the size of the group grew. All new poems were displayed on the bulletin board each month for our residents to enjoy, then they were placed into a book that was created and developed as the class grew. This booklet still sits in our library for all of the residents to view. It's titled "Poet's Corner Originals." There are at least three hundred original poems written by over thirty-five residents.

Opera Buffs

Dr. Manhueser owned all of the operas known to man. Pavarotti, Leontyne Price, Plácido Domingo, and José Carreras were just a few of the famous opera singers in his personal library of CDs and DVDs. Each month, Opera Buffs would meet in the large activity center and view famous operas while having wine and cheese at a candlelight table. *La Traviata* by Verdi, *Carmen* by Bizet, *Die Zauberflöte* by Mozart, *La Bohème* by Puccini, *Tosca* by Puccini, *The Barber of Seville* by Rossini, *Rigoletto* by Verdi, *The Marriage of Figaro* by Mozart, *Don Giovanni* by Mozart, and *Madama Butterfly* by Puccini were some of the many wonderful operas that we were blessed to see, thanks to our Dr. Manhueser!

Dr. M was fascinated by the game of croquet. He was a very good player, so we made him captain and coach of our team. He would hold croquet workshops to teach residents how to play and how to improve their skills and be competitive while playing. Most residents got upset if their ball was hit by another player's ball, or they would pass the opponent's ball and miss an incredible shot to avoid an argument. This made Dr. M go crazy! He did not believe in "good manners at croquet." This man was competitive, and as he taught croquet workshops, others became competitive as well. The men had no problem hitting the opponent's ball, but the ladies were not so daring.

There was one lady, Nettie, who did love the game and wanted to beat Dr. M. She would practice almost every day for an hour, and finally her hard work paid off. During a spring tournament, Nettie and her partner played in the finals with Dr. M and his male partner. After an hour of play, Nettie hit the post in the middle of the field to end the game and win for her team.

She yelled out, "I finally beat the man at his game!"

Dr. M left the field that day in silence. We think he was a bit upset.

As I write this book, let it be known that Dr. M is still with us to this day at 103 years young. Yes, that's the truth. He gets up around 6:00 a.m., walks every day for about an hour, and reads and listens to his operas during the day; and before he goes to bed around 8:00 p.m. or 9:00 p.m., he walks down to the dining room to pick up his meal, which is usually by 5:00 p.m. Each week on Tuesdays, he rides the bus to our shopping mall; then on Thursdays, he goes to the local grocery store. We all pass by him in the hallway with a high five, and he gives one back in return with a wonderful smile.

OUR PIANO DUO

In 1992, the year I was hired at the ANNH, there was a small group of residents who sang old favorites every week led by one of the nuns. This nun retired, so it was easy for me to step in and lead the group. Playing the piano was not an easy task for me, but singing came easy. A note was placed on the bulletin board asking for a piano player. In just three days, a dear sweet resident came to my office volunteering for the position. Mrs. Birch could not hear a sound, but she played the piano like Liberace and knew every song in the Baptist hymnal as well as all of the songs from the '30s and '40s. During her younger years, she was a piano teacher and played for her church for about twenty-five years. The music group was so excited to have this very elegant and super talented lady as our pianist. Word spread throughout the village, and our attendance grew every week. We decided to become a mission choir and sing at other nursing homes and retirement facilities that were close by. Our name became the Angel's Nest Nursing Home Sunshine Choir with twenty members and a gifted pianist. Once a month, we traveled to another facility and began our program with Elvis Presley's "Blue Suede Shoes." Our group had no inhibitions; so we each spray-painted an old pair of our shoes bright blue and gave a smashing opening number with tapping, clapping, and singing Elvis! We would include patriotic and Broadway songs, but we would always end our program with "God Bless America" and "Till We Meet Again." Tears and smiles came from all of our audiences, and we all swelled up on the inside and shed some tears too.

After a year with Mrs. Birch by our side, another talented pianist/organist moved into the Nest. Mr. Smith was from New York, and his reputation as a famous organist from the St. Clement's Episcopal Church came with him. Mr. Smith had played there for twenty-five years, but because he was over seventy-something, he decided to move into the Nest where the priest from the St. Clement's Episcopal Church had come to retire. Several of St. Clement's members and clergy joined these two over a period of three years. New York was coming to the South, and we were excited about it.

I was walking down the hall near the living areas one afternoon and heard a beautiful sound coming from one of the apartments. It was Mr. Smith's for sure, and the music mesmerized me to the point of almost being frozen. My ears had never heard such sound coming from an organ. My hand went to the door and knocked before I could stop it! Mr. Smith opened the door, and there I stood with my mouth wide open. This man was very shy, and he blushed when he saw me. The compliments kept coming out of my mouth, so he invited me in for a miniconcert. He had an organ on one side of his living room and a piano on the other side. We had a very interesting conversation following his playing, and I learned that he loved to play piano duos but had no one to play with. Mrs. Birch came to my mind instantly, and he agreed to meet her if she was willing. It only took two weeks for these two talented folks to begin playing music together. Mrs. Birch loved all of Mr. Smith's selections, so they never tired of playing some of the world's most popular pieces, from Beethoven to Mendelssohn. The beauty with this couple came from Mr. Smith taking Mrs. Birch's hand and patting the rhythm before they began playing. She would pat it back on his hand to be sure it was correct. Then the music would come and flow through the fingers of these senior musicians. The two gave a concert every month that lasted over an hour; and the room was full every time with residents, friends, and family members of Mrs. Birch who would all be in shock and disbelief when the concert was over. These gifted pianists shared their talents with the world, and we were beneficiaries of their gifts.

THREE'S A CROWD

It always amazed me to witness cupid at work just about every day at the Nest. Lovebirds were everywhere, and it reminded me of my high school days and even junior high crushes. Every time a new man moved in, or an attractive lady, the buzz would begin. My office was opposite the indoor resident mailboxes; so I heard most of the conversations, which, in most cases, I did not care to hear. It wasn't a matter of eavesdropping but rather a resident getting carried away with his/her story or gossip tales.

Gus Black moved into one of our Grande apartments. There were only three of them, and the monthly fee was pretty steep since the Grandes were constructed from two regular apartments made into one. Each had a fireplace, washer and dryer, and two full baths. Mr. Black retired from a major soft drink company as president and CEO with a truckload of achievements that preceded him. He was a singer, dancer, and golf pro and had given to all the major charities in the sum of a few million dollars. His sister lived at the Nest, but she never exposed her brother until he had completed his final move and was the guest at her dinner party held at the local country club.

A few of the lovely ladies from the Nest were invited to this dinner, along with a couple who knew Mr. Black from their days of traveling with him and his late wife. Mr. Black had covered all of the world except Africa and Australia, which he made plans to see in the near future.

One of the ladies became a stalker and followed Mr. Black into dinner, sat by him during daily activities, and called him on many occasions to dine with her. Being the gentleman that he was, Mr. Black was very gracious to accept dinner invitations from this lady, whom we will call Alice. Now, if my facts are correct, Alice was a very wealthy lady whose husband had invented a sugar substitute that is still in restaurants today in a little pink or blue or yellow packet. I will not give the exact color out for this specific sweetener. She came to the Nest with her sister and had given a great sum of money to build another wing onto the nursing home for total nursing care patients. She was very generous but a bit commanding when she wanted specific repairs or additions to her apartment done in a timely manner. We tried to meet her needs and gave her the same attention that was given to all of our residents.

One fine day in the spring of the year, a beautiful lady from Canada came to live with us at the Nest. Ina

Anderson was a renowned artist who brought her beautiful oils with her and donated many of them to the new wing being built and several to the refurbished lobby entrance. She was a poet and could recite all of Robert Browning's poems. She even painted many of his poems through illustrations on canvas: *My Last Duchess*, "The Boy and the Angel," "A Pretty Woman," and "Easter Day" were a few of her selections.

There was an activity each month called Dinner Out where the residents would ride the bus to a different restaurant in the area. Ina went with the group for one month and sat at the table with Alice and Gus. It didn't take a rocket scientist to figure out the instant attraction Gus had for Ina. He was a smoker, and Ina hated smoke. Gus started to light a cigarette in the restaurant (when smoking was not outlawed), and he looked at Ina to see if the smoke would bother her. She replied that the smoke was fine, and it even smelled delightful. Cupid was hitting her smack in the face, and we all saw it happen! The next day, Gus and Ina were having lunch together. Alice was at the mailboxes screaming her lungs out that she was gonna kill that stupid woman when she could get the chance. At that moment, Ina and Gus passed her with a nod, and Alice just smiled back at them. The romance between Gus and Ina spread like a hurricane over the Atlantic Ocean. They were in love and inseparable. Everywhere you saw Gus, you saw Ina. Trips were taken to the Orient, Africa, and Australia with only the two of them from the Nest going. Once, Gus took his sister and her husband with them to Hawaii for a week. Pictures were on the bulletin board the next week, showing favorite places from Hawaii with the lovebirds in each photo. When I came to work the next day, after the photos were put on the bulletin board, I saw one of the pictures with tack holes all in it (just on the face of Ina). Before anyone else could see the doctored pic, it was taken down. Junior high school days came to mind, and I laughed inside at the foolishness of it all.

BESSY AND BT

Farming came to the Nest when Bessy and BT moved in. This couple came with farm tools including a tiller and lawn mower. It was very important for them to start a garden, so a place was set aside for their garden spot and more spaces for residents who wanted to grow a crop of vegetables or flowers. The garden club caught on instantly. More than twelve residents wanted garden spots, so maintenance took BT's tiller and two-by-fours to create four-feet-by-eight-feet spaces. This small area was not enough for Bessy and BT. They were determined to have a large garden. Mr. Whit agreed. He was a gardener too and wanted space for his tomatoes, corn, and daylilies. A tree was cut down to give the gardeners plenty of sun so their crops would grow. Blueberry bushes were planted, and Mr. Pat even put in an asparagus bed. Mrs. Betty planted rosemary, and in just one season, there was enough rosemary for the entire home. In two seasons, there were enough blueberries for anyone who would go and pick them.

Mr. Pat finally got tired of asparagus, so he offered the crop to anyone who could cut it and weed the bed while there.

One summer, the Nest had a contest to see which resident could have the prettiest and most clever decorations at their apartment entrance. Each apartment had a shelf and space for a chair or table at the front door. All of the residents decorated their entrance to give passersby an idea of who lived behind the door. Some entrances had family pictures. Some would display beautiful ceramics or silk flower arrangements, and some even had very expensive paintings and vases on their shelf and wall. The theme for the contest was Southern styles. This could be anything and everything relating to summer in the South. Almost every family entered this fun and very interesting contest. The judges for the event were the officers and the council members of the residents' association. Twelve judges would go to each entrance and give a blue ribbon to the first-place winner and several red ribbons and yellow ribbons for second and third place. Bessy and BT went to their garden and picked all of their ripe vegetables, put them in an old and very large basket, and made a sign which read "The South's Finest." Bessy was convinced that their display would win; so she told everyone that, after the contest, she would hand out all the vegetables to anyone who wanted to eat them.

It took the judges about an hour to look at all of the wonderful entries.

The winners were posted on the bulletin board after lunch, and all of the residents gathered around when they heard Bessy yelling from the hallway, "Hell no! We didn't get second place. We got first place, dammit, and I am keeping all these fine vegetables!"

Guess what we didn't do the next year?

MESSAGE FROM ABOVE

Each year, the Sunshine Choir gave an early morning Easter sunrise service at 6:30 a.m. in the courtyard for all of the residents and their family members. A priest or a denomination preacher was asked each year to give a fifteen-minute message following the choir's well-practiced Easter songs, which might include "The Holy City," "Jerusalem," "He Arose," and, a favorite that they sang every year, "Gethsemane."

Father Jeff agreed to come one year and give the message. He was a local priest whom we all loved. His father was a Baptist preacher, so Father Jeff knew a ton of Baptist hymns. On many occasions, he would come to our choir practice and sing bass with the men. Sometimes he would sit at the piano and play hymns, drawing a group of folks in to sing with him. He was very young and energetic. The folks would smile and join in with him as he told his jokes and sang favorite songs to the residents.

On this particular Easter Sunday, Father Jeff came early to set up a podium and help move the electric piano onto the courtyard. I would always arrive around 5:30 a.m. to be sure our maintenance men were gathering extra chairs for outside or adding more chairs inside due to inclement weather.

This was going to be a beautiful sunrise service. The sky was pink, orange, blue, and purple. The sun was scheduled to rise just about the time Father Jeff would bring his message. All of the sisters came from the convent, and the dining room had delivered the hot sausage and biscuits and orange juice to the coffee shop adjacent to the courtyard. Coffee was plentiful, but the food would stay under cover until the service was over. Everyone would stay and enjoy the sausage and biscuits with blueberry jam and cold orange juice, and they would fellowship with one another until it was time for all to go to Mass or leave on the bus for the service at the local Baptist church.

The choir sang their selections straight to God because the harmony was so perfect. Even the men stayed on pitch, and our two tenors rang out on key. Father Jeff began his message, and all eyes and ears were fixed on him. He talked about the blessings of our Heavenly Father, and he named a few of the blessings all around us.

As he began to say, "Even the birds of the air bless our Heavenly Father," a flock of thirty to forty geese flew over, quacking so loudly he stopped in the middle of a sentence, looked up at the birds, and said, "It took us two weeks to get that right!"

The crowd roared with laughter, and we ended the service with "Praise God from Whom All Blessings Flow."

MOMMA 2 AND MOMMA 3

One of the beautiful things about working at the Angel's Nest Nursing Home was that most of the residents would treat you like family. They quickly became so attached to you that it was hard to think of them as acquaintances but rather kinfolks.

Momma 2 was a perfect example of being more than a resident. When she came to the Nest, it was pretty certain that she was gonna attach herself to me and become my shadow, in a good way. She had so many talents that it was hard to know what she couldn't do. If there was a special activity, she would make a poster for it and put the announcement on our bulletin board. If a new resident moved in, she would send them a handwritten note with artwork on it. She was an artist, and she loved arts and crafts. It didn't matter what it was; she could make it, stitch it, or paint it. Nothing was impossible for Momma 2. Evelyn got her name Momma 2 because she bossed me around in a sweet way on every occasion. Daily critiques were given to me before she and I called it a day.

The display case was her responsibility after she told me it was important for her to take on that task. I gladly agreed and gave her all rights to the thing. Each month, she would create a new theme and display dolls one month, veterans with pictures of them and their families one month, art from our artists, rare antiques that would fit in the display case and descriptions of each unusual piece, and even knife collections and clock collections. Residents would volunteer to bring his/her collections; and one month, Momma 2 had a Christmas nativity scene collection and, one year, a Santa Claus collection. Each month, conversations at the display case were common because there was much to talk about when the case was complete for that month.

Momma 2 loved to come out to our house and pet our dogs. She loved animals and adopted my husband and our eight dogs. Just about every month, she would bring my husband a painting or a pie and treats for the dogs. We were not allowed to accept any gifts from the residents, so she got around that rule by giving my husband and our dogs special gifts. Once, I tried to give the painting she had done of birds, which was in a beautiful gold frame, back to her; but she became furious and told me that the painting was not mine and to mind my own business. She drove off in a rage! I stopped trying to "mind her business" after that.

There was never a kinder, more loving lady than Momma 2 unless it was my Momma 3. Anna Claire was Momma 2's best friend who had worked with her in the same office building for twenty years. Anna Claire moved into the Nest about a year after Momma 2 had graced us with her move. The name Momma 3 came from Anna Claire because she was jealous that Evelyn had been given that special kinship. Neither one of these ladies had children. So they both doted on me all the time, and I loved it. Momma 3 could cook as well as Momma 2, and about once a month, my husband and I would have these two precious mommas over for a meal and a long visit. Usually, it would be around Thanksgiving and Christmas that the two of them would make the visit last for about four hours or more. The time would pass by so fast, and waving bye to us, they would promise to come back very soon and bring more banana pudding and coconut cake.

In the spring of the year, these two mommas called and said they had to come over with a surprise. When they arrived, we were blessed with two azalea bushes. These were planted in our backyard and named Momma 2 and Momma 3 so my husband and I would never forget our mommas! It would be impossible to forget these fun ladies.

During a tornado warning, we all went to the hallway in our house and sat for about an hour. Momma 3 said it would be glorious to be blown into heaven with these special children, as they called us. God spared us that night, and all was well for a while.

The choir was a special place for my mommas. They never missed coming to practice, and Momma 2 sang in a quartet several times during the years she was with us. She even led several art classes, especially during the holidays, creating Christmas ornaments and beautiful hand-painted Christmas cards. Momma 2 loved to decorate, so she was the chairman of the hall decorations and chose themes for each hall every Christmas. It was a winter wonderland when Momma 2 was at the Nest. Momma 3 would help as much as she could. But her walking skills were not as good as they should be, so she used a walker (rollator) most of the time. She would paint and help Momma 2 with all of her creations, so the dynamic duo always came to the rescue with every event.

The most rewarding time for these mommas was when a group of grade children came to teach the residents how to paint a flowerpot and plant an herb in the painted pot. This was something the school wanted to make happen so the children would have exposure to older adults. There were at least fifteen children, so we had fifteen residents in order to pair off and participate in this activity. Before the class had finished, Momma 2 and Momma 3 had the children painting butterflies on the pots and teaching them a different way to plant with moss instead of dirt. The kids were having a blast, and my two mommas were in heaven. The school sent a letter the next week thanking us for allowing the grade the opportunity of being involved in a well-planned and successful event, hoping they could make this an annual affair. That did not happen. Momma 2 said those kids were clueless!

LEAVE IT TO LAMAR

"A new man is moving in! Come on, ladies. Let's see what he looks like!"

Thirty screaming crazy ladies went down the corridor and into the main lobby just to get a glimpse at the new guy! He was coming to the Nest from Birmingham, Alabama, driving a white Mercedes and carrying a retired military tag on the front of this fancy vehicle. I think we had over thirty curious spectators hanging around the front yard and playing croquet on the side yard when our new man finally arrived. The band did not play, but the noise was very noticeable. Lamar pulled up in the front-covered vestibule and began blowing his "bugle" car horn.

He jumped out of the car, waving at everyone and yelling, "I'm here, ladies! Get ready for me. Here I come!"

All of the crowd gathered with haste to meet this new character called Lamar! He greeted each lady with a kiss and a red rose! Yes, I said with a red rose! This man was prepared and ready for these piranhas, and he caught them all by surprise!

Dashing into the dining room for dinner was a sight to see because all of the residents, including the married ones, were waiting to see this new man, Lamar, make his grand entrance for the first time into the elite and very formal dining room of the Angel's Nest Nursing Home! Most of the residents gathered to eat right at 5:00 p.m. even though the dining room was open until 6:30 p.m. It seemed that, if you were late, you might not have enough food to eat; so everyone acted as if it were the last supper! An hour passed, and no Lamar! Folks were anxious, bored, and restless at 6:00 p.m. when the new guy finally made his first appearance! First there was awe, followed by several gasps of air, then concluded by one lady fainting at her table. Lamar made his grand entrance. He was wearing shorts, tennis shoes, and a casual pullover shirt. He waved at the crowd and asked to be seated alone. Some folks waved back, but most of the residents just gave him a shocking stare with red faces and mouths wide open!

Our Lamar never wore long pants to the dining room. He never was asked by a single lady to breakfast, lunch, or dinner. He never was invited to go with anyone on an excursion or day trip. Lamar picked his own lady friends and men friends, and he traveled across the country about every six months and always took several guests with him of his choosing. This man was extremely unique in every way. All the folks at the Nest began to warm up to his charm and hospitality. He started a trend for sure. Almost all of the men, especially the single ones, wore shorts to the dining room; and many of the men began courting ladies at other retirement facilities. A calm was had at the Nest!

BACHELORS NEVER WENT HUNGRY

The village people were always having parties in the activity room and down their halls. Usually, everyone was invited to the event. It was very unusual if all of the bachelors were not present. Because the ratio of men to ladies was three to twelve, our men were always the center of attention. If a man wasn't invited to dinner after the party, he was invited to breakfast in the Cyber Café the next morning! Pairing off was not the norm because the men enjoyed the attention of *all* the single ladies, seeing that each lady competed to make the best cake, the best casserole, the best lunch, the best dinner; or the most times, she (whoever she was) had a male companion to accompany her to every event. If she had a different male companion at each event, it was considered that this Southern lady was a very wealthy and/ or attractive female for sure! Some of the residents came from other states like New York, Minnesota, Wisconsin, and Michigan; but they were usually a married couple with family ties in the area.

Hunger pains did not occur with these bachelors! After each party, the single men would get takeout containers and fill them full with leftovers! The ladies would be sure that these men were filled to the brim and were loaded down with plenty of food for the next meal! I dare say that our bachelors were not frail and thin. They were the epitome of contentment and happy souls smiling with satisfied palettes!

The bachelors had plenty to eat; and their wallets were not challenged due to the fact that the single ladies kept them occupied at the village or, many times, on very expensive excursions, all expenses paid as long as the two went as a couple. One particular bachelor B went on a weeklong trip with Ms. A. Things were going pretty well until bachelor B started flirting with a younger woman on the Greek island of Antiparos! Ms. A became so upset with bachelor B she booked a private plane and headed back to the Angel's Nest Nursing Home, leaving the poor bachelor B stranded on the remote island. As I recall, this poor man didn't come back for a month. The word was he had to find a job washing dishes at one of the island cafés until he had enough airfare to get home. I don't believe he ever left the grounds of the Nest again!

BINGO! NO! NO! IT'S GAMBLING!

Hard-shell, foot-washin' Baptists were only a few of the different faith groups at the Nest! We had just plain Baptists, Methodists, Whiskeypalians, Episcopalians, Presbyterians, Mormons, Jewish faith, Church of God, and Catholics! This group mixed fairly well with each other most of the time. There were several occasions that required some quick thinkin' and super planning on my part. The bingo and casino stories will give you some kind of idea about what I'm talking about.

One bright, sunshiny morning, Mrs. Algood, a Southern Baptist, came rushing into my office with a panic-stricken look on her face and with a body trembling from the top of her sprayed hairdo to the bottom of her penny-loafer heels. I jumped out of my desk chair and rushed toward her. She threw that right arm up and blocked my approach with a body stance that made baseball catchers blush!

"You've got to stop playing bingo! You've got to stop immediately! It's gambling, and you will all go straight to hell! And you have got to stop taking these sinners to the casino! That's gambling too, and it's got to stop! I feel it is my duty to warn you right now before the Lord calls you all and sends you to hell," she announced.

I told her that this was quite a lot to take in at once, so I would need a day or two to let it all soak in and asked her to come and see me in a few days. She agreed to do so. I then immediately called her son, who had been to many of the activities here at the Nest, and told him exactly what his mother had said to me and in what manner she had said it. He laughed and laughed and assured me that his momma would be changing her tune posthaste!

On Friday morning, Mrs. Algood came singing into the office with a smile that Ajax couldn't remove! She told me to sign her up for bingo and handed me her $1 for a bingo card, and then she told me to put her name down on the list for the next casino trip! I almost fell out of my chair and asked her if she would repeat what she had just said. She told me that her son had given her some play money and that everyone over the age of sixty-five needed some play money because no senior adult would think of gambling at his or her age! She skipped out of the office and never missed another bingo game or trip to one of the casinos. By the way, we all received free lunches, free transportation, and $15 in play money from the casinos!

OUR TWO MUSKETEERS!

It was the year 2015, and in my mind, the thought of retirement seemed to be creeping into my brain on a regular basis. The workload was about the same. But we were adding residents in patio homes every month, and there was a waiting list of over eighty-five families wanting to get into our lovely Nest!

I was in the activity center at noon one beautiful spring day when I heard two voices say, "Shirley Sunshine, sign us up! We are ready to play!"

These melodious voices came from a couple we will call the two musketeers! Roy and Mendy had just retired from sales and nursing, leaving their five children and their families in other states. They were ready to join every activity we had and create some new ones! This rare and wonderful burst of energy coming from both of them lit a fire under me that is hard to explain or even impossible to recreate! The smile on my face is still there, and their energy and enthusiasm for life are still flowing all over the Angel's

Nest Nursing Home today! As a matter of fact, they are still bouncing all over the place as I write this story!

I can honestly say that this couple, being seventy-five and seventy-eight years young, would even make two kids who are eight and ten look older than the two of them! The energy and love that they gave us all will always be felt at the Nest!

Several examples were the following: After every event, Roy and Mendy stayed and cleaned up and put up every chair, table, and material to make ready for the next activity. They always came early to "help" with whatever was needed and to make my tasks easier. I couldn't retire! There was too much fun going on. These two musketeers were causing the place to get energized with tons of laughter and residents volunteering to help too, and new activities were added because of the talents these two brought with them. Roy and Mendy joined the Sunshine Choir; Dinner Out Club; Bingo Callers Group; Happy Hour Hostesses; Coffee Klatch; Travel Club, going on every trip we planned and being the first two to sign up for every trip and activity that required a signature; morning exercise; Walk Around Mississippi Club; and more!

They brought decorations for the Super Bowl parties each year with the two teams' jerseys, footballs, napkins, and balloons, along with food, food, and food! At the New

Year's Eve party, this couple greeted everyone at the door with horns and hats and a glass of champagne! They were definitely party animals that I had only dreamed about, but this dream actually came true!

I was not about to retire! *Retire? And miss all the fun? No way!* One day, we were having a sing-along in the activity room for our St. Paddy's party. I happened to hear a beautiful tenor voice. It was Roy! He was harmonizing to the tune of "My Wild Irish Rose"! After the party, as Roy and Mendy were leaving, I mentioned that it would be so much fun to have a couple sing some of Hank Williams and Patsy Cline songs at the next party. Roy immediately volunteered, and Mendy said for me to be Patsy Cline! She would share Roy with me because he loved to sing, and she loved to listen!

The plans began, and we became Hank Williams and Patsy Cline. I told Roy that he was an answer to prayer because we had a resident some years back who sang with me as Hank Williams and even sang "Ave Maria" in Latin.

He was Bill Basken and his wife, Sue, loved to hear him sing; so she gave her permission for us to "cut up." Roy reminded me so much of Bill because he would try anything and not hesitate one second! These men loved to live and share their talents with the residents! Roy and I became the concert duo and even went to other nursing homes to perform. Sometimes the choir would be present, and other times, we would be asked to sing and have lunch with the various groups. Some church senior citizens found out about Hank and Patsy, so we went to at least one church or retirement facility each month for quite a while. Our faithful instrumentalists always went with us: Patsy, Al, and Helene stuck by us and made us sound like pros!

Live wires and electric bolts were only a few descriptive words for this so-special couple! Roy and Mendy have always been giving themselves with time, money, and talents that will always be remembered by so many at the Nest. The elementary schools in the area have been blessed by them as well. Each school year, they go as Andy and Raggedy Ann and read children's books to the children each week. Sometimes they dress as dinosaurs or whales to emphasize the characters in the book they are reading. What a fun life they have, and what a wonderful way they have exposed themselves to us! We are still being blessed, and I added two more years before I retired so I could soak in their warmth and laughter! Yummy!

PICKWICK WILL NEVER BE THE SAME!

Our travel club group loved to go off on some wild excursions and explore new places. With a trip overdue, we planned a three-day to two-night run to Pickwick Lake for some beautiful scenery and wonderful catfish! News spread fast, and we had to limit the number of residents to thirty-two due to the bus that we booked ahead of time. It would only hold thirty-two passengers, and all other busses were contracted out for the big golf tournament held in our area every year. Folks from all over the country would be at this golf event, and many of our people went as spectators and volunteers. With that nationally known tournament going on at the same time as our trip to Pickwick, we still had a waiting list for this most unusual adventure up north to the wilderness country (or so I told them) for the first week in October.

As we traveled toward our destination, the bus was filled with smiles and stories and jokes told by most of the residents. There was plenty of time to talk about memories past and even tell a few jokes that seemed to make everyone laugh. We kept them PG in content since there was a morning devotion and prayer each day we journeyed. The Lord knows we needed His guidance, so we tried to behave most of the time!

When we arrived at our motel, the smiles dropped to frowns until each resident realized that every room had a balcony overlooking the river and the dining hall was big enough to serve the armed forces! The meals at the motel were very delicious and very Southern; no complaints there from any of us! After breakfast on day two, we headed to the dock where a large paddleboat was waiting for us. We were to tour the Pickwick Lake and have our bag lunch on the double-decker paddleboat. The weather was perfect with a slight breeze to keep us comfortable but not too cool. The lake tour lasted about three hours, leaving us filled with beautiful nature scenes, animals and birds of all kinds, and full stomachs from a great lunch catered by the motel.

We had just enough time to get back and take a shower and a short nap before we journeyed to our out-of-civilization café for dinner that was about twenty miles up a winding mountain trail called a road but looked like a mountain path. The bus was able to travel on it with great caution. We were told that there would be no traffic because this was a very remote café that served reservations-only folks. That was us all right! We had made the reservations at least a month prior to the trip; and the menu was to consist of quail, duck, and venison with vegetables and cornbread added. Beer and wine would be served with tea, water, and coffee. We always had teetotalers and wine drinkers on every trip, so the menu sounded very appealing to the majority of this fun crowd.

Leaving the motel at 6:00 p.m. would put us at the out-of-civilization café around 7:00 p.m., we thought! This winding road kept winding and winding until I thought we were headed to the wilderness unexplored! Finally, we pulled up to this café around 8:15 p.m. I had called ahead to say that we were coming but didn't know if we were lost. The reply was to come on and not worry because we were not lost. So we kept coming! This café looked like a tornado had been through it and over it and around it. The roof was barely on, or so it seemed. But the sign was lit like the Fourth of July and said, "Welcome to Civilization Again. Come on in!"

I always went in to scout out the vicinity before the group, and this time, it was *shocking* to see the inside of this deserted café. One man was there, who was to lock up when the reserved party was finished. The cook had left;

and there was no waitress, hostess, or other living soul to be found! Of course, this called for plans B, C, and D!

Preparing our group for this catastrophe was going to be quite a challenge! As they entered the what's-left-of-a-building, I explained that we were very fortunate to have the entire place to ourselves and that we would have an experience that would stay with us for some time! My husband jumped right in and became the bartender, along with two other men in the group. Father M went to the jukebox and began plugging quarters into the machine that actually worked! With music, cold beer, and bottled water, we were on a roll! Now where was the food to feed these very hungry folks who had not eaten since noon? Thank goodness we had a couple with us who had owned a restaurant, so they ran to the "kitchen" to find hot dogs and french fries. They went to work with those, and I found key lime pie in the freezer enough for all of us! We had most of the line dancers with us, so they started the "Boot Scootin' Boogie" while everyone else joined in. The party had begun. Smiles were on every face, and the beer kept coming. After Father M had his fourth beer, he said it was time for comedy hour. Well, let me just say that this comedy hour was hilarious with Catholic jokes that only the pope would have told to his cardinals! Even the custodian was right in the middle of our party laughing along with us! He said this was the most fun he had had in years and didn't want us to leave!

We were very blessed to have plenty of hot dogs, coleslaw, and french fries for everyone! Key lime pie was a big hit as well! We used paper plates, plastic forks, and paper napkins and threw it all, including the beer cans and empty bottle water containers, in the trash can with a note:

> Noting your absence, we thought it best to journey on. Thank you for the complimentary food and beverages. It saved us from starving. Please keep the $100 deposit for a tip to give to the custodian. He is a saint! The $200 is for beer and pie!

On our third day, we had lunch on the river at a famous restaurant that featured all-you-can-eat catfish and homemade banana pudding. We enjoyed our last dining experience almost as much as we did at the crazy out-of-civilization café!

ART CLASS TO
THE MISSISSIPPI
MUSEUM OF ART

We were in dire need of an assistant in the independent-living area, which was my neck of the woods. My CEO told me to get some help! I asked if I was to hire someone part-time or full-time. She said to hire a full-time assistant if we needed to.

Well, folks, for eighteen years, there was no part-time or full-time helper, except for the wonderful residents who would volunteer to help with *everything* and, on many occasions, cleaning up after a big party or picking up after an outside group had come to perform, with a catering request for food to follow! Those events were our largest in attendance of around 200–250 folks with standing room only. The setup would take several hours, and the cleanup would take as long as it took, even until midnight if needed. We had a few very dedicated residents who stayed until all was done, but it was time to give them a break. We needed an assistant!

After interviewing over twenty applicants, we hired a lady who was my age and who brought bridge and art to the Nest! We needed bridge tournaments, and I couldn't even spell bridge, much less play the game! Biddy Bee was perfectly capable of teaching bridge, playing bridge, holding bridge tournaments, and bringing over sixty-five players into this one activity. She was a ball of fire! We needed her, and we got her!

Her other wonderful talent was art! I don't mean crayons and construction paper! I mean watercolor on canvas, oils, acrylics, charcoal, and pastels with the ability to teach a blind man how to paint! Biddy Bee was our answer to many prayers at the Nest. We were very busy all the time, but to have this artist and bridge instructor in our midst was almost a miracle! In no time at all, Biddy Bee had over fifty art students who met every week and were eager to meet any challenge our art teacher put before us! We, including myself (this was in-service training for me), bought all of our materials, including our medium in paints ranging from pastel chalks to Grumbacher oils. Biddy Bee told me that, if we owned our materials and paid for them with our own money, we would take charge and not miss any of her classes. She was right! We had twenty-four to thirty-six beginners and around ten to twelve ladies and men who had taken art or who had become artists in their earlier years. Biddy Bee knew just how to teach us all because her concepts and methods were extremely clear, precise, and exciting. She would paint the project at home, then bring it to class and paint with us in front of the room.

This method was wonderful, and we were spoiled to it until about a year after we had started these classes.

She challenged us to paint an original to show at the Mississippi Museum of Art. We could enter two paintings that she would approve of, and they would stay in the museum for about a month. We were so excited and thrilled to be a part of this awesome and challenging project. Biddy Bee made us work like Hebrew slaves before we could sign any of our work, especially the two pieces we would show at the museum. We had four months to complete this task, and we were able to meet twice a week in order to finish on time and make a really good showing for the Nest!

The big day finally came. Fifty-two artists represented our Perfect Palette Art Group with over one hundred original paintings in oil, acrylic, pastels, and watercolor. We were pumped and dressed to perfection with bold colors to match our artsy personalities. The entire village made it to the museum on several day trips. On the last day of showing, the museum, along with the mayor of the town, gave us a beautiful reception; and our group picture was in the local paper. I don't think we came off of cloud nine for many days that followed. Several of the art students sold their work to outside observers and to many of our own residents and family members. Art at the Nest was one of the finest activities we ever accomplished with the fabulous instructions from our Biddy Bee! We all miss her!

A FOND FAREWELL
BUT NOT GOODBYE

There are hundreds of stories that could be told at the Angel's Nest Nursing Home and most assuredly at other homes for older adults as well. These are just a few of the tales that were true, and I hope I brought smiles and a few laughs as you read them. The joy and fullness of life that older adults bring to those they meet show us all that there is an abundant life to be had until the Good Lord calls us home! These precious senior adults showed me and much of the world how much fun one can have by jumping out of our comfort zones and trying new things that make for a better world in the lives of so many! It's not the risks we take that make life worth living but the time we spend with others sharing our talents, gifts, personalities, and love that our blessed Savior has given to each of us! Life is precious and truly a gift to share! Thank you for spending some of your time with us at the Nest!

By the way, our Punch Line Theatre Group created seven wonderful plays that we will share with you in the next book to come in the near future! Stay tuned for some more laughs and crazy times from the Angel's Nest Nursing Home residents! Until we meet again. May God bless you and keep you in His arms!

ABOUT THE AUTHOR

Sam Mym will remain incognito for now, but many folks who read this book will know without a doubt who she is. A dedicated athlete, assistant activity director at a Baptist church, teacher, coach, executive director and trainer for a national cosmetic company, activity director for a retirement facility, women's Bible study teacher, motivational speaker, choir director, and soloist are some of the opportunities she encountered over the years. Playing gospel music on the piano was and still is a blessing!

Her BA in education and MHA in health care have served her well in the various fields of interest, allowing her to consult employees in time management, consensus training, and workers in the field of health care.

In 2000, she created an organization to help health-care workers and activity coordinators with their day-to-day tasks as they worked with senior adults. She realized that programs and activities for senior facilities were lacking in many areas such as enrichment classes in education, history, the arts, computers, social skills, music, photography, better health, and physical, mental, and spiritual growth. By bringing together health-care workers once a month to network and share ideas, the programs they planned at their facilities could be improved, and the residents would reap the benefits. The success of this organization has flourished throughout the state where she lives. Many of the shared ideas and programs are still implemented in facilities today.

CPSIA information can be obtained
at www.ICGtesting.com
Printed in the USA
LVHW030121180422
716363LV00001B/70